Buddhist Meditation

Buddhist Meditation

VENERABLE SAMDHONG RINPOCHE

wisdom tree

First published 2010
Reprinted 2011

ISBN 978-81-8328-177-5

Published by
Wisdom Tree
4779/23, Ansari Road
Darya Ganj, New Delhi-2
Ph.: 011-23247966/67/68
wisdomtreebooks@gmail.com

Printed in India

CONTENTS

EDITOR'S NOTE

Samdhong Rinpoche is the head of the Central Institute of Higher Tibetan Studies at Varanasi. From infancy, he was given the rigorous religious and philosophical training suitable for an incarnated lama in Tibet. He came to India in the retinue of His Holiness the Dalai Lama in 1959 when the Chinese occupied his country.

This little book is based on a series of talks given to students at the School of the Wisdom at Adyar in 1982. It soon became evident to those who heard them that the speaker was sharing his own deep experiences of meditation without in any way wishing to impose his own preferences and views on others. There was an atmosphere of simplicity, and indeed of contemplation, that did more, perhaps, to convey the spirit of meditation than the words alone could accomplish.

Editing of the material has been kept to a minimum in the hope that readers will catch something of the same atmosphere and be inspired to go deeper into this important subject.

We wish to express our special thanks to Miss Carin Citroen for her patience and care in transcribing and typing the talks.

Editor

1

MEDITATION: ITS PURPOSE, MEANING AND PREPARATIONS

I am not an expert on Buddhist meditation. If one does not himself know how to sing, how can he teach another? However, let us attempt to come to some understanding of the subject. Let us begin by considering two basic questions: What is meditation? Why do we meditate? A sensible man takes on an assignment only after proper consideration of the means and the likely outcome. To start something without this does not seem to be wise.

It is true that people are intelligent enough without meditation. Science has developed beyond our expectations without meditation; the computer operates much more rapidly without meditation than the human brain that built it. Why then should we concern ourselves with it? Our innumerable births have already heavily conditioned our minds; surely they do not need further conditioning even through meditation! Why are so many people nowadays eager to meditate? In some places it is more difficult to find a good teashop than a centre for meditation—or at any rate, a centre where it is taught!

And what is the result of meditation? People have meditated for years and yet they seem to be as human and miserable as those who have not. It is not my purpose to discourage you from meditation, but I mention this in order to draw your attention to this fact so that you may think about it yourself. For if you find meditation a useless exercise, it is better to do something else.

My first question to those who want to meditate would be: Why do you want to do it? I consider this question very important, for it is the intention which decides the entire value of the meditation. If our motivation is not as pure as it should be, it is our duty to correct ourselves by right thinking. Some people want to meditate because they have a disturbed mind and they want a peaceful one. They do not know what a peaceful mind is or the real nature of peace. They want a kind of peace which is restful and can produce the same effect as deep sleep; this has no connection with wisdom. They only want to be free from their restlessness, or their tiredness, or their frustration. It would be better for them to take a couple of sleeping pills for these not only work faster but produce the desired result without any effort on the part of the sufferer. Other people think of meditation as a kind of therapy for curing physical and mental diseases and although this may happen occasionally it is not its primary function. Modern medicine with its chemical remedies and techniques has far greater efficacy in this field.

Then there are those who want to gain magical powers or some sort of special powers that feed their already enlarged egos. They want something uncommon that ordinary people do not have—just to show off, in fact. For these people meditation will be an utter failure; it may even divert them into immoral activities.

We should be very careful, then, and examine our motives as to why we want to meditate. And first we must know what meditation is. For our two questions—why do we meditate? What is meditation?—are closely interrelated.

I do not know the derivation of the English word 'meditation', but in Sanskritic tradition meditation has two aspects, *dhāranā* and *bhāvanā. Dhāranā* means to concentrate and *bhāvanā* to ponder, think upon, investigate, analyse. So real meditation must consist of these two parts—one-pointedness of mind and the power of analysing. These two together form the totality of meditation that is *śamatha* and *vipassanā. Śamatha* is to concentrate and *vipassanā* to analyse. Analysis with total concentration makes meditation. Now, what do we concentrate on and what do we analyse? Generally, in the outer world one does not need a concentrated mind, a fullness of mind, in order to analyse.

Even the scientist, without meditating, and depending

only on outer instruments, has analysed the material world with great skill. But he has left untouched the inner self. The truth of the inner side of things cannot be explored by scientific methods or equipment. The existence and the importance of the spiritual dimension are gaining more acknowledgements in the present day. Earlier, when science was developing, most people thought that spiritual things and the inner wisdom were irrelevant. But now scientists themselves are realising that there is still something to be discovered, and that perhaps, it can only be done by some method which is beyond materialism. Meditation is concentration and reflection and these must be inward, not outward. Meditation is the instrument that we need in order to go inside ourselves to search for that which is yet beyond ourselves.

Methods of meditation are to be found in most religious writings. The Buddhists have no special methods which could be described as purely Buddhist. But they have several insights that are specifically their own; for instance on the nature of *śamatha* or calmness of mind, and *vipassanā* or alertness of mind. But the techniques are derived from those known in the Sāmkhya, Vedānta and other Hindu schools of philosophy, and perhaps in other religions which teach meditation.

Our mind, as it is, is really not qualified or equipped to search into the innermost depths of ourselves. We have been given guidelines as to how to search for things outside ourselves but hardly any directions have been given on how to look inwards. We have to train ourselves to look inside, and the only way to achieve this is through meditation. In order to meditate, the mind should be channelled, otherwise it will not have the power to concentrate on one object. In that case, what we often imagine to be meditation is not meditation at all. Our undisciplined mind is like a candle flame which flickers in the wind. Objects distorted by such a light seem to be vibrating and cannot be clearly distinguished by the eyes. Even a few moments of meditation make one realise how quickly the mind moves from one object to another and how disturbed it is by many causes such as emotions and memories. The mind resembles a crowded street in which cars, motorcycles, bicycles and people are moving. When we are in the crowd we are aware only of the rush and fuss around us, but if we look down from the top floor of a tall building we shall see how large the crowd is and how numerous the people. Similarly, when the mind is full of disturbance and obstructions we do not notice how fickle it is. When we start to meditate and are able to detach ourselves, we become aware how crowded and restless the mind is. The mind of the ordinary man is usually fragmented and divided, full of thoughts and illusions. In this condition concentration is absolutely impossible. Thus, in order to look inwards, so that we come to know our inner selves better, the mind must be trained in concentration.

The first step in meditation, then, is to train the mind to concentrate on one point, one object, for a definite period of time. This is in order to overcome the limitation of our present mind which can neither concentrate fully on one object nor remain concentrated even for a little while. For example, while we are talking, our mind should be fully concentrated on the subject under discussion. But actually, only a part of it is attending to what is being said, for at the same time we hear the sound of a bird outside and notice the movement of the people about us. The mind, then, is doing several things at the same time, such as listening, seeing and speaking. This shows clearly that it is seldom able to concentrate on one point only, although sometimes the opposite is true. For instance, it may happen that when we are looking at a beautiful picture or at a sunset, we become so absorbed in it that we fail to hear that somebody is speaking to us. This kind of concentration, however, usually lasts for a few seconds only and then all is gone again.

The first step in meditation, then, is to train the mind to concentrate on one point without being distracted or disturbed. But we shall soon notice that due to the intense and continual exercises in concentration, we are apt to lose our ability to analyse and think. It is very important not to do this because, while concentration is the first step in meditation, thinking, pondering and analysing is the second step. It is on these vital activities that meditation is built, namely, one-pointed concentration on a subject or object, and the retention of the ability during concentration to see clearly and ponder its many aspects. If this is understood we shall understand what the Buddhists mean by meditation.

Now we shall go back to the reason for meditation. Meditation will only be useful and worth while if we are really serious about finding ourselves, or if we are, in Buddhist terminology, 'searching for our selflessness' or 'searching for that which is illusive within'. If we are in earnest to find that truth—not for our own satisfaction, but in order to help other people who have not found it yet—then it is well worth while to study meditation and to practise it. But if our motivation is not pure, meditation will just be a waste of time, for it cannot be used to serve any worldly aims such as the obtaining of pleasure or power.

The world is full of wretchedness. Nobody can deny it. Our bodies are subject to decay, disease, pain and death. And there are the miseries of the world such as poverty, inequality, hatred. Every single person whether well-known or unknown, rich or poor, young or old, carries his own bundle of misery—his body—to which he is bound by karma. A sensible person should not only recognise the immense misery in the world but should also enquire into its cause. According to a Buddhist doctrine, misery is caused by karma which is conditioned by pleasure, the product of an impure mind. This impure mind is created by the illusion of the self, *avidyā* or ignorance. The illusion of self can only be eradicated by *prajñā* or wisdom or the understanding achieved through *samādhi*, the concentrated mind. And the concentrated mind can only be achieved if we have observed *śīla,* the moral or righteous way of living. Therefore, the entire Buddhist teaching is summarised in *triśikshā,* the three doctrines—*śīla*, *samādhi* and *prajñā*. It is clear from this that meditation becomes indispensable for anybody who tries to achieve right understanding of Truth, the realisation of Truth, the realisation of selflessness or of Self as it is. Thus, we should meditate in order to develop our mind and attain an insight into the inner nature of man. We must have a fully concentrated mind which we shall achieve through right meditation.

Having defined meditation and discovered why we wish to meditate, we might now look at our preparation for meditation. Preparation is very important; it can neither be overlooked nor neglected. Buddhist meditation is in three stages. The first stage is study—to hear from your instructors and seniors, to study books and discuss your findings. Therefore, *śruti,* to hear (understanding by hearing), is the first stage. This is followed by the second stage which is *vichāra,* to ponder, to think over what has been heard and whatever explanations you have received. Then you have to consider carefully whether the methods you are about to use are correct and are suitable for your own particular condition. Only then, when your mind is made up and you are definite about the methods you are going to use, can you go on to the third stage which is *bhāvanā,* to meditate.

There are also certain conditions which are absolutely necessary for a beginner. For instance, he must have a suitable place to live in. It must be calm and quiet, a place where he can sit without fear of intrusion, without mental stress or uneasiness, conscious or unconscious, for fear of any kind is the end of meditation. It should also be reasonably near to the market or shops so that he may easily obtain his food, clothing, medicine and other necessities. In the early stages, an isolated place is not advisable. To have to travel for miles to a doctor would be a waste of time which the meditator cannot afford, especially at the beginning of his enterprise.

Our lives should be clean, physically and, especially, morally. We must be content to live a simple life, subduing our desires for luxury. We must stop thinking about obtaining better, more, or newer gadgets and other goods, because all these thoughts disturb and distract the mind. We should learn to be satisfied with what we have, whether it be food, clothing, or the place we live in. The fully advanced meditator can do as he wishes, but it is best for the beginner to turn away from outer objects altogether such as watching television, going to the cinema, reading newspapers, or moving through busy streets.

In order to further curb and quieten the mind we should give attention to our daily routine. This means rising, eating, sleeping, and so on, following a strict timetable. We must also eat simple food in moderation, preferably pure vegetarian. Finally it is important to understand that living a clean life means that the livelihood of the aspiring meditator should never be involved with immoral earnings. A person who has been comfortably settled in one place for a while and has seriously practised this routine should find that his body and mind have largely calmed down.

From what has been said, it will be seen why a busy executive or, for that matter, any busy person living a hectic life, attending public meetings, rushing from here to there and working at all hours, will not be able to prepare for meditation. The necessary calming down is not achieved through meditation, but by living an ordinary routine life. Even technicians and scholars will find it difficult to start meditation, as meditation and research do not combine well together in the beginning, certainly not for the first three to six months or so. However, if the technicians and scholars are advanced meditators they should have no difficulty whatever in doing their work and meditating as well. But to start with it is better to give up all those varied activities that are not helpful to one who wants to practise concentration. Moreover, it is advisable for the beginner to possess only a few books and these should deal with the subject of meditation only. Besides his books it is also to his advantage to have a teacher or congenial friends so that if any doubt arises about the methods he is using, or the ways in which he is trying to improve his meditation, he can discuss it with them.

When all the above preparations are completed the aspirant should review his entire life. He must examine again his intentions, his understanding of what meditation is, and why it is he wants to meditate, because he must now decide either to give up his desire to meditate, or to go in for short periods of meditation only. He must also re-examine his environment and the preparations he has made. It cannot be emphasised too often that meditation is not easy and can often become dangerous, leading the slipshod meditator into an abnormal life. All these precautions should therefore be taken by those who wish to enter into a serious meditative life, who are in earnest about wanting to achieve a more spiritual way of life and to search for Truth.

If a person is not in a position to undertake protracted and regular meditation he should take a limited course and that will also help him to a great extent. He could go into a retreat, from a few days to several months. It is important that he should decide on the exact duration of such a course so that there will be no uncertainty about it in his mind. The curriculum should be properly planned and the programme should be drawn up so that at the end the participant will have achieved something, such as perhaps a better understanding of meditation.

After having attended two or three courses the meditator will perhaps be able to start out on his own and undertake a little longer meditation without the constant help of a teacher. However, it must be understood that the beginner needs a great deal of help in the early stages of his development, notwithstanding his own studies or the instructions he has received from his teacher, or how confident he may be about the methods he is using. It is therefore advised that the aspirant should discuss his progress with his teacher or fellow aspirants from time to time, because a wrong method of meditation adopted at the beginning and practised for a lengthy period may prove harmful.

Questions And Answers

Q. You spoke about clarity and alertness of the mind and also about concentration and analysis. What do you mean when you speak about analysis as a part of meditation? I ask this because you started by saying that the mind is crowded with so many thoughts and that analysis is an activity of thought. Therefore, does not the process of analysis crowd the mind with more thoughts?

A. That is a very important question and it has been discussed at length in the Buddhist *Śāstra*s or scriptures. The Buddhist *āchāra*s (techniques) may be divided into two parts. The first one is *vipassanā*, to think, to analyse, and the second part is *śamatha*, to concentrate. Many *āchārya*s or teachers recommend *śamatha* only, for meditation, and do not refer to *vipassanā*. But there are also well-known *āchārya*s who advocate that the two aspects should go together in meditation. *Śamatha* is the calming down and concentration of the mind, while *vipassanā* or analysis is a process of thought. In the ordinary mind this process is neither concentrated nor fully channelled, while the analysing process of thought during meditation is fully concentrated and channelled.

Thought will not jump from subject to subject while it is under discipline. Moreover, the meditator chooses only one thought for his analysis and in this context analysis means the searching of the self to find out whether it is an entity or a projection of the mind, whether its nature is interdependence and 'avoidance of is-ness'. Unless we analyse and ponder this we cannot find Truth. In the first stage, the realisation of Truth can only be reached by *anumāna,* inference. *Anumāna* is, of course, thought, but when one progresses in meditation, *anumāna* or inference, becomes less and less necessary. Thus the part which thought plays in the meditative process gradually diminishes until it fades out completely when one obtains *pratyaksha* or direct realisation. The process of thought is now not crowded but systematic and one-pointed, as there is only one subject to be analysed. Therefore, with full concentration of the mind, analysing will be sharp and forceful. In this way the process of thought is used to eliminate the thought processes.

Q. *What about the use of prāṇāyāma in meditation?*

A. *Prāṇāyāma* is commonly known in Buddhism as concentration on the breath. But the *prāṇāyāma* prescribed in Hindu yoga and the breathing tradition in Buddhism are meant for different purposes. In Buddhist meditation, we just count the breath as it goes in and out of the nostrils and we concentrate at the same time on the tip of the nose. Breathing has an effect on the physical body, and this in turn helps us to bring the mind under control. In Mahāyāna Buddhism many beginners start their meditation by concentrating on their breathing instead of on an outer object, and this concentration on the breath purifies the body as well as the mind.

Q. *What is the role of mantras in meditation?*

A. Mantras are sometimes very useful in the higher stages of meditation. In Buddhism, they are only used in Tantric meditation, not in ordinary meditation. Meditation normally begins with the training of the mind. Tantric meditation, however, begins with the combined development of mind, body and speech, all three together. This being the case, mantras (involving speech) are indispensable.

2

TIBETAN MEDITATION SCHOOLS, THE NOBLE EIGHTFOLD PATH AND POSTURES

There were several dozen different schools of meditation in Tibet, each with a different tradition and approach. It is not necessary to discuss them all. Instead, because it is important for us to be clear-minded, we shall consider one tradition only, namely the Vijñāna-vāda school of Mahāyāna Buddhism which was founded by the teacher Asanga. This, and the Mādhyamika school, are the two best known schools of Mahāyāna Buddhism. Together they represent the two aspects of the *prajña-pāramitā* sutra. Asanga commented mainly on the *mārga*, or meditational side, while the great teacher Nāgārjuna emphasised in his commentaries on the *darśana* or philosophical aspect of it.

The Asanga school of meditation was very popular in Tibet and had many followers. It has come down to us through an uninterrupted line of gurus, enriched by oral teachings, invaluable treatises and commentaries of such great men as Āchārya Vasubandhu, Śāntarakshita, Kamalaśīla and Tson-kha-pa. It is the method of meditation given in the writings of these *āchāryas* that we shall study.

Let us now continue with the subject of preparation for meditation. Since correct preparation is the very foundation of meditation we shall study it stage by stage.

Although there are some other systems that are less demanding, in this tradition there are no short cuts, no relaxations or concessions as regards moral discipline. It is very strict about physical and verbal disciplines and expects the student to be really serious about his approach to meditation, because until he has disciplined himself in body and speech he will not be able to discipline his mind. The accepted method of discipline in this school covers three stages:

- *Kāya,* discipline of the physical body.
- *Vāk,* discipline of speech.
- *Chitta,* discipline of the mind.

Thus, in order to discipline the mind we must start with disciplining the physical body and then the speech. After these two have been fully brought under control we find that the mind can be disciplined easily.

The Buddhist way of life is based on the Noble Eightfold Path. This Path consists of the disciplines in the above three stages. Right action, right intention and right livelihood together constitute the moral part of life or *śīla*, while right effort and right mindfulness are the components of *samādhi*. A right outlook on life results in *prajñā*. Right action, right intention and right livelihood should be observed in the first stage of one's preparation for meditation, *samādhi* and *prajñā*. If the intention is right, all else can be achieved.

Anything started with a wrong intention will be wrong, however good the ensuing action appears to be. Similarly with meditation also: if the intention is wrong, impure and selfish in nature, although we may use a good method, all that follows will only strengthen the self and the result will not be right. A good intention, then, must be established at the very beginning and then we must discipline body, speech and mind. So, right action, right speech and right livelihood must be practised at the second stage of our preparation.

Most of our activities are involved in one way or another with our livelihood and so it is necessary to examine our way of life with care. It includes all the activities we engage in such as earning money and spending it, as well as simple things like cooking, eating, sleeping, and the way in which we react to others. Naturally, we are concerned about how to earn a satisfactory livelihood, but our efforts to do so can lead us into immoral activities. Most of the crimes of which we hear or read in the newspapers arise from the desire for money. Sometimes it is very difficult to follow right livelihood under the present conditions of society. Even a person who is normally honest may at times find himself tempted to dishonesty, or to engage in wrongful business activities. These things happen. But if we look at ourselves closely and carefully, we shall find that we do not always detect our own mistakes or wrongdoings, or if we do there is always some reason to excuse ourselves.

It is a good exercise to scrutinise our actions honestly and sincerely. Look at ourselves when, for instance, we make a train journey, when we receive our salary, or when we use special privileges. Can we say that we are completely clean and honest? Can we say that we earn our money by absolutely fair dealing with full application of ourselves to the work? Our means of livelihood may be clean and there may be no dishonesty or wrongful earnings. But if we look at our work carefully we may come to see that a number of wrongful actions are involved in it. For example, we are expected to work for a certain period of time every day. We may indeed stay in the office for the full number of hours but, looking closely at what happens during these hours, we may find that a fair amount of time was not spent on the particular job we were supposed to do. Then there is the question of the use of office stationery. How many times, unconsciously perhaps, do we put office paper, or pins, or envelopes to our own personal use? Similarly, what about the use of the staff car? There are rules about its use but we often find that these instructions are not always followed and that the car is booked for trips which, strictly speaking, it should not have made.

Similarly, the office telephone is meant to be used for office business but in fact it is sometimes used for purely personal purposes. It is in ways like this that our means of livelihood become somewhat polluted.

Another example can be found in the market where, perhaps, we always try to get the best article at the cheapest price while the seller, in his turn, tries to sell his worst products for the highest rate he can get. For many, it is almost impossible to reach the standard of perfection demanded by right livelihood, but we must keep on trying. The *samskāra* is always changing and there is no doubt that if we try hard enough we shall be able, in the end, to achieve the highest standard.

Right speech is as difficult as right livelihood; our words do not always conform to our thoughts. Conversation has become an essential part of our society. It is very difficult to keep our speech clean: we find that about half of our usual conversation arises out of conformity to social customs. This is the reason why, in the old days, teachers chose the path of silence and kept a lifelong vow not to speak because they realised how much impurity can be involved in speech. There are many occasions when our educated, civilised society would regard it as most impolite if we were to tell the truth, and so we have to twist our speech a little. Sometimes, when this twisting is done with a good intention, it may not be too bad, but often the good intention is lacking. For example, let us take a person who usually rises late in the morning. One day he is disturbed by somebody who comes to see him early in the morning. This irritates him, but nevertheless he gets up and meets the visitor with a smile on his face, saying: 'I am so happy to see you.' Saying what he really thought would be regarded as most impolite, but, at the same time, what he said was utterly untrue. In like manner, according to our custom, we have to carry on from morning to night an artificial and formal conversation—whether we are in the street, in the market place, in a bus, or attending a meeting—for the sake of being regarded as a civilised and well-mannered person. It was for this reason that the ancient *āchāryas* said that the only person who speaks the truth is a madman because he always says whatever he thinks!

Next comes the purity of right action. We act and react very often totally automatically or involuntarily. Our thoughts are so conditioned, our speech so swayed by the instant reactions of our mind, that much of our action is an involuntary expression of the condition of the mind. For instance, how many actions do we perform thoughtlessly and without attention? And even if we do give them some consideration and thought they are still often wrong. Therefore, the attainment of control by purification of body, speech and action is an absolute prerequisite before we can start to discipline and control the mind, otherwise the difficulties we face are too numerous and varied and it would be impossible to cope with them all at once.

If a person has succeeded in disciplining his actions and speech and in engaging in right livelihood, he has become quite a spiritual being without the use of meditation. Meditation is really not absolutely necessary if one is able to keep oneself strictly to this discipline: this manner of life so uplifts a man that it is well worth while to reach such a standard, if not in this life then perhaps in the next. The best thing for us is to keep on trying, even if we fail now and then. If we fall, we must just get up and push on, aiming at the same goal.

Right livelihood, right speech, right action and, first of all, right intention are the four disciplines which have to be implemented in order to prepare the ground for meditation, while discipline of body and speech are specifically required in order to discipline the mind. Besides all this, quietness and nearness to Nature are very helpful, not only for meditating, but also to prepare ourselves in general. If we live in a quiet place it will be much easier to practise right action, right livelihood, right speech and right intention. Noises create the worst kind of disturbance for the mind. Spiritual music (*bhajans*) and prayers can be used either at the beginning in order to build up a religious atmosphere, or at the end of the practice, but the beginner is advised not to use either of these practices during his meditation for they do not help in concentration. At a later stage, however, concentration on sound and listening also becomes a part of meditation, but this is not easy.

The next step in meditation is the practice of *āsana*s or outward postures. Everybody knows about them for they are common to all systems of meditation. The disciplines of mind and body are very much correlated, for the mind functions through the body and brain. In Vajrāyana, they begin with control of the physical body and thus they control the mind and still its movements. However, it is a highly intricate and secret system and only a few selected people are able to follow it. The body is the vehicle of the mind. If we compare the body to a car, we can see the relationship clearly. If the car stops (if the body is brought under control), the driver (the mind) comes automatically to a halt also. Therefore, as the discipline of the mind is of great importance so is the use of good posture. The postures or *āsana*s which are generally advised for meditation may not suit everyone, and every person should find out for himself which sitting posture suits him best. There are, however, a few basic principles which should be adhered to. First, during meditation, whether we sit on the floor, on a chair, or whether we stand or move around, our spine should be kept absolutely straight. We must watch it carefully because many of us have the habit of stooping a little while sitting or standing. There may also be a few people who are not physically able to keep their spine straight and these will have some difficulties to overcome at the beginning, but I am sure that if they practise regularly they will be able to sit straight. Then, it is also essential that our breath should be normal, which means that our body must be relaxed.

We should never start to meditate when we are tense or tired. People who have reached a higher stage in meditation can meditate while running, driving, swimming—in fact they meditate under any circumstances. But in the beginning we should strictly adhere to the conditions laid down in order to make the practice easier. The most common posture is the one where we sit on the floor on a mattress or on a cushion which is slightly higher at the back than in the front. We can make this by folding a blanket into a slightly slanted position. The slant makes it easier for us to keep a straight back and it is more comfortable for those who wish to sit for a long time. However, many people are accustomed to sitting on a chair and it may be unsuitable for them to sit on the floor with legs crossed. That is all right: it is not a new method; in ancient times there were also those who sat in chairs while meditating. The chair should not be too soft so that we sink down in it. It should have a firm seat on which we can sit with a straight back, our feet resting comfortably on the floor. If we wish, we can also meditate while walking slowly and concentrating on our steps.

In any case, the one condition which prevails in all these positions is to keep the back straight. The position which people often find very difficult to master is the Vajra-paryānga Āsana. This is the Buddha posture where the legs are crossed so that the feet rest upon the upper portion of the thighs, the soles turned upwards, the right leg being on the outside. It is useless to strain yourself in order to force the legs into this position. The reason for sitting cross-legged is to make it possible to meditate for a prolonged period, but if you have to strain yourself, you will feel pain within five or six minutes. So do not worry about adopting a particular position. If you want to sit cross-legged on the floor, do it in a way that is easy and normal to yourself. The soles of the feet do not have to be turned upwards if you cannot do it, but the spine should be straight, the head slightly bent forward, and the hands should be resting comfortably either on the knees or in your lap.

There are also a number of positions recommended for the hands. One often used in Tibet is to place the left hand in one's lap and the right hand on it. The palms of both hands should be turned up with the tips of the thumbs touching each other. Another is to put the left hand in your lap with the palm up and rest the right hand, palm down, on it. This is the posture of humility. Again, another is to rest the hands on the knees, the left hand on the left knee and the right hand on the right knee, and let the fingertips just touch the floor. Or the hands are laid down in one's lap, the thumb of each pressed against the fingers. But this position is not comfortable and should not be used if one wishes to meditate for a longer period. The following position of the hands is an aid for anyone who wishes to slowly straighten the spine; it is therefore not a posture but a help. Fold the thumbs inside the hands and then press the hands in the groin.

In former days, students did not start to meditate straightaway, but practised first of all the different postures for several weeks to find out which suited them. So, first of all, find that posture—sitting, standing or moving about—which is most suitable for comfortable meditation. Similarly, some hand postures may suit some meditators more than others; some may be more useful for a person sitting in a chair while others are more suitable for those who are sitting on the floor.

The next important point to be discussed is the eyes. In the Buddhist meditation system it is never recommended to close the eyes during meditation. Many people in the beginning may feel that they must keep their eyes closed, but shutting the eyes or ears does not help one to concentrate better. If the half-open eyes prevent us from concentrating, we may darken the room, but the eyes should not be closed. They should be looking down in such a way that the edge of the nose is just in view. But do not stare at your nose, because that is no good and will give you a pain in the eyes. You should look down effortlessly in such a manner that the tip of your nose is vaguely visible. Then, the mouth and teeth should be considered. The teeth should not be clenched, neither should the mouth be open. Retain throughout a relaxed and natural condition of the muscles and make yourself comfortable in the meditation position you have chosen. If you do that, your breathing will be normal and quiet and this is important. If it is not, you should wait until it is before you start your concentration. Now after sitting quietly in the meditation posture for one or two minutes, begin to concentrate on your breathing by counting the breath going in and out for at least twenty-one times. This exercise will put the whole of your bodily system in order. Later on, you can start concentrating on the object of your choice.

Breathing should always be through the nose. Breathe out slowly, breathe in slowly, and do not hold the breath beyond what you are normally used to. Mentally count: 'I am breathing out...and I am breathing in...that is one; I am breathing out...and I am breathing in...that is two' and so forth. This exercise is not real concentration but rather an accurate following of your breathing pattern. But it will release you from contact with the outer world; that is to say, you will forget the other things you had in your mind because your thought is now wholly on counting the breath. In this manner you clear the way, or make a track for the mind, which leads to concentration. You may, if you find it helpful, count the breath a hundred times or four hundred times. In any case, this exercise will give you immediate relief from mental tension and physical strain and will therefore calm your mind and body. Today, this particular exercise is used by many people solely for the purpose of relaxation. They lie down or sit in a chair and watch their breathing until it has gained, or regained, its normal pattern; then they start counting it and that refreshes them. It is necessary for the beginner to do this exercise before he starts his concentration.

We have touched on just a few of the prescribed conditions, the preliminary steps leading to meditation. Once again I must stress the importance of living a benevolent life—

with or without meditation—always keeping the intention pure, and speech, action and livelihood clean. Anybody who achieves this standard of living is a noble man, whether he meditates or not. Always, at the base of all lies our intention. If we could constantly examine ourselves at every step we take we would definitely find a great improvement in our life after only a month or so.

Many people think that all this is only a theory because, they say, the conditions in the world are such that we would not be able to survive if we were to be 100 per cent honest. I personally do not agree with this statement but you will have to find out for yourselves whether it is true or not, and you can only do so if you earnestly try to live the life.

If we live a clean life and maintain this style of living over a certain period we shall find that our surroundings and circumstances will yield to us and that those elements which were originally, perhaps, of a contrary nature will change so that they now harmonise with the way we live. If we have the will to try it, it will be worth while to carry out this experiment at least once or twice in our lives, and we shall find that somehow we receive encouragement to continue. In this way, as we become purer, we shall little by little improve our lives so that it becomes easier for us, and we shall find fewer conflicts and contradictions obstructing our way. This will strengthen the mind and give it more stability.

These practices are not mere theories; they should be an integral part of our daily life. Besides, what is the use of meditation if we do not care to practise the preliminary steps? Meditation by itself cannot transform us all of a sudden. We have to set ourselves a task and adhere to it, proceeding step by step. If we want to travel, we must depend on a vehicle, but once we arrive we do not remain in the vehicle. It had only a temporary use for us and now it has served its purpose. We leave it and go straight ahead. Similarly, all who aspire to meditate must depend on many prescribed rules, exercises and conditions which have been tested from ancient times and proved to be absolutely necessary as preliminaries to meditation. The beginner should adhere strictly to them but later on he can leave them behind. And it may perhaps be good to remember that wise men have said that, a whole life spent only in preparation is very worthwhile.

Questions And Answers

Q. *You mentioned at the beginning the* mārga *side and the* darśana *side of the* prajña-pāramitā *sutra. The* mārga *aspect was commented upon by Asanga and seems to be a method for meditation. The* darśana *side, you said, was commented upon by Nāgārjuna. Is the* darśana *aspect also a method of meditation?*

A. *Darśana* means philosophy. The Buddhist tradition consists of two parts: one part is meditation and the other philosophy. The philosophical part was expounded by Nāgārjuna, and the meditation part by Asanga, who was regarded as the expert in that particular field.

Q. *You said that the eyes should not be closed during meditation, I personally find it more comfortable to close them.*

A. If you find it uncomfortable or perhaps impossible to meditate with your eyes open, then, in order to help yourself in the beginning and to avoid closing the eyes, you, can make the room dark. Closing the eyes during meditation is not recommended.

Q. *Is keeping the eyes open not prescribed to prevent one from going to sleep?*

A. That may, of course, be one reason. But the principle behind this rule is that meditating with closed eyes (which may be easier for a beginner) disturbs the meditator when he reaches a more advanced stage.

Q. *Must one keep the eyes completely open or half-closed?*

A. One just looks down on the floor, right in the front. You may call that keeping the eyes half-closed. Do not look into the distance when you are meditating.

Q. *When you keep your eyes open, do you focus them?*

A. No, do not focus the eyes, because that will strain and tire them. Just keep the eyes half-open without trying to look and direct them downwards on the floor in front of you.

Q. *Would you say that a different effect is produced on the mind by keeping the eyes open or dosed?*

A. Yes, there is. As I mentioned before, if you start meditating with your eyes closed, you shut yourself off from seeing things and therefore it will be less difficult to achieve concentration. But then, if for some reason your eyes open during meditation, you will be disturbed. That is why it has been recommended to meditators to keep their sense organs awake and open.

Q. *You said that if one's purity increases, the environment will yield to one. Would you please enlarge on that?*

A. You will find that there is nearly always a struggle between the individual and his environment. If the environment affects or influences a person, then that person is weak. A person who is able to make his own environment is strong. Great people who live in a bad environment often lift the environment up by their mere presence and turn it into a good place. In that case, the environment has yielded because the purity of the person which is radiating out from him influences the environment and it is elevated by those vibrations. If one is pure enough, I am sure that one can cope with the problem of one's environment; otherwise one will find it difficult.

Q. *I understand all that you have said and it is obvious that one has to reach a high standard of purity. But what is pure and what is impure? There seem to be no hard and fast rules. It is difficult to decide what would be the pure and correct action to take at a particular time.*

A. Yes, it can be a problem. According to Buddhist teachings, whether an action is pure or impure, right or wrong, is measured by its violence or non-violence. Any action which directly or indirectly causes harm or violence to any sentient being must be considered impure. An action which brings no harm to any sentient being is regarded as a normal action. An action, which is helpful or beneficial, directly or indirectly, is considered to be a pure and right act.

Q. *Shall I speak the truth to someone when I know that it will hurt him? Would not this also be an act of violence?*

A. This is often difficult to judge. If by hurting someone you are indirectly helping him, then you should hurt him. But if it is not going to help him, you should avoid it. Every case has to be judged on its own merit; if your intention is correct and pure, your judgement will be correct and also your speech. It may happen occasionally that by not speaking the truth you can help a person. That is quite all right, too, and the proper thing to do. Take the case of a person being pursued by another with intent to kill him. You may be there and see the fugitive disappearing into a certain house. The pursuer, who has lost track of his victim, comes to you and asks you whether you saw him and if you did, where did he go. Would you tell the killer the truth? It is a matter of discretion. If one's intention is pure and selfless, wisdom will be achieved sooner or later.

3

OBJECT AND METHODS OF CONCENTRATION

We shall now deal with the object and methods of concentration. A beginner's mind is so conditioned that he cannot focus it wholly without the aid of an object to concentrate on; he needs a method, or a teacher.

The object to be chosen for concentration in this system of meditation—which is the achievement of *śamatha* and *vipassanā*—will differ from person to person. Each will have to choose his object for himself, according to his preference, and whatever is most convenient for him. Naturally, all these instructions and guidelines are only for those serious students who want to meditate until the real *śamatha* is achieved. For casual meditators who only want to follow a course for a couple of weeks or so, the decision about a suitable object can be made quickly. But one who wants to achieve full concentration must take great care in the choice of an object, for if a wrong decision is made the entire meditation may go wrong.

Generally, the objects to choose from fall into two groups. The first consists of those objects or points to concentrate on which affect the nature of the inner body, while the objects in the second group affect the outer body. The concentration on breathing and on the movement of the breath, and concentration on the mind itself belong to the inner body group. A person advanced on this path might start, right from the beginning, to meditate on the mind itself. This would be of great benefit to him at a later stage also, because sooner or later we all have to meditate on the nature of the mind. That meditation will be our highest aim. But, for beginners, this sort of concentration is difficult because to make a picture or image of the mind is well-nigh impossible. It is for this reason that other suggestions have been given with regard to choosing an object for concentration. To concentrate on the movement of the breath is a good alternative for some people. The breath is closely related to the well-being of the body, and if chosen as an object for concentration it holds the attention of the mind quite easily. But it also has a difficult aspect because it is constantly moving. However, when it moves, let the mind move with it. In other words, synchronise the movement of the mind with the movement of the breath and you will find that the nature of this very movement will steady the mind.

Then there are those who like to focus their attention on the rising and falling of the chest as they breathe in and breathe out. And there are other ways of concentrating on the breath, but we need not now go into those details.

The other objects related to the phenomena outside the body may also be divided into two classes, namely the group related to sound and the group related to forms. In the former, the meditator concentrates, for example, on the sound of a particular *akshara* or syllable such as the sound of *A* or *Aum,* and makes a mental picture of that sound. He does not hear the sound, but concentrates on it. In the latter, he makes a mental picture of, for instance, a deity, or perhaps just a *bindu* or point (like, a point of light), that is neither too bright nor too dull. It is not necessary that the meditator should have an image of his deity as a point of concentration, but some people like it. Buddhists generally recommend an image of the Buddha for the beginner, for it not only serves as an object for concentration but at the same time it reminds us of the Buddha nature. Actually, any kind of picture can be used as an object for concentration, but once the choice has been made we must persevere with it and not change it until *śamatha* is achieved however long that may take.

In all cases the object for meditation should be chosen carefully. For example, a person who is very much influenced by his *rāga* or attachments, should choose an ugly object for which he is not likely to develop a passion or attachment; a person who is easily angered should make a mental picture of and concentrate on the pacifying beauties of Nature; a person who suffers from constant and rapid movement of thoughts should choose an object which does not involve much thinking. Another method for finding the right object is to go by natural preferences. For example, some people are more attached to bright objects, while others may prefer dark ones. The tendencies and nature of each person should decide his choice.

In any case the object has some psychological relation to and effect on the one who concentrates on it. Therefore instructors never prescribe the object for concentration nor are they rigid about the type of object. There is a story that in ancient times there was a person who could not concentrate on any object however much he tried. So one day his teacher asked him: 'What did you do when you were young?' The man replied that he had been a cowherd and looked after big buffaloes. 'All right,' the teacher said, 'why do you not concentrate on that? Why not concentrate on the head of a big buffalo?' The story goes on to say that the man followed the suggestion of his teacher and happily achieved *śamatha.*

The object, then, can be, a part of the body, or it may be an object apart from the physical person. Whatever it may be, its real value lies in its mentally projected picture. For instance, if a person chooses an image of the Buddha as his object it is not the outer image in itself that he will meditate on. He may look at the object beforehand, or when he starts his concentration, but the real object he is going to meditate on is the picture of that image in his mind. The thought or the memory of an image is not an object. But if we can produce a well-defined picture of the outer image in our mind (whether it be an image of the Lord Buddha, or a deity, or a syllable, or a point of light), that is the real object of meditation. The *Śāstras* also mention that only the *pratibimba* in our *citta*—the picture of the object within our mind, not seen by the eyes, or heard by the ears—is to be recognised as the real object.

The choice of an object is so individual that no one, not even an instructor, can give advice. But, by practising experimentally on a different object every day we can eliminate those that are not suitable for our purpose, and finally choose the one on which we are able to meditate for a fixed period of time.

When you have made a choice among those objects which you think will fit the purpose, you take that object and experiment again by concentrating on it to see whether you can remember all of it in your mind. If the mind becomes scattered or if it grows sleepy, the object is not suitable. But if you feel that your whole mental force is alert and active when you think of the object and recall it, then it is right for you.

You must now decide on the size and colour of the object. Some people prefer a small object and others a large one. Again, you must experiment and make the necessary adjustments. The usual advice given to a beginner is that the size of the object of his concentration should not be bigger than his own body. If, for example, he wants to concentrate on a tree, he should reduce its size to his own body measurements. On the other hand, it should not be smaller than what can easily be seen by the naked eye.

The next aspect to be taken into consideration is the colour of the object. Black is not considered to be good, but any other colour is suitable. It should be chosen according to one's taste and, again, one should try out several options before a definite choice is made. If one chooses to concentrate on sound, this should be chosen in the same way as regards forms. The final choice in all these things always rests with oneself. Having decided on the object, the next decision to be made is where it is to be placed and at what height, for this is also important in our efforts to achieve concentration. For some people it is helpful to place the object low—sometimes lower than themselves—while others like it placed high. In general, it is advised to place the object in a manner so that one can look at it without raising or lowering one's head.

Now comes the question of how to make a picture of the object. Suppose you would like to make a picture of the Buddha's image. In this case, you should have an image near you, and before you go into meditation you should take a good look at it. Then you close your eyes and try to recall what the image looks like. After a while, open your eyes and look again at the image, and then close them and try to recall it once more.

Keep on repeating this process until you get a clear picture of the image in your mind. When that has been achieved you should stop looking at the outer object. In the particular system of meditation which I am discussing, there should be no object near the meditator once he is able to picture it clearly in the mind.

From this moment, our exercises in concentration start. We must now consider how to focus our mind and concentrate, and how to open up and direct our full attention to the object. Concentration on an object during meditation is not thought, in the ordinary sense of the word, neither is it perception. It is direct contact, a total focusing of the attention on the object. To achieve an undivided mind is difficult for a beginner because he is not yet able to discriminate between thought and meditative attention. Meditative attention often comes under the cover of thought and so we sometimes need thought in order to start us off. Everything to the point where the object was chosen is a process of thinking, but meditative attention directed to the object means very much more than merely thinking about it.

Let us now go over the process of concentration again, step by step. You look at an outside object and hold the memory of it in your mind. Then try to build file memory into a clear mental picture. Up to this stage you have only used thought. But now comes a change; you leave thought, and the picture rests in the field of the undivided attention of your mind.

Thought is a moving process; it cannot remain focused on one object for long. This is the reason why thought distorts the picture and therefore whatever your thought and mental images may be, they are always very different from what really is. Thought only represents your own interpretation of an object, or of whatever it is you see. For example, in thinking of a certain person, your thought never touches him, for the real person is never in the thought process. At present, we cannot do anything about this confusion as we are under the spell of this kind of imaginative mental activity. If we were to shut out all thought so that we did not think at all, we would not sufficiently perceive the world around us. Moreover, our whole personality would be shattered and we should be unable to function properly. Without the thinking process all our activities would come to a standstill because our actions are influenced and guided by words and thoughts.

We give names to everything that comes to our knowledge or within our view. This naming or describing of events and experiences is a useful means of classifying and arranging whatever we register with our senses, within the limited framework of our understanding. It is because of this that naming becomes important to us. This means that we actually cannot perceive anything *as it is,* for a mind which functions within such a limitation is not an open one. Therefore there is no real communication but only a relative connection between *what is* and the storehouse of memories, words and classifications within our mind. Our whole personality is drowned in this activity of the mind and so we float helplessly in a sea of imagination and illusion.

Buddhists speak about a two-tier system of relative truth and absolute truth. As we have just seen, we live, act and behave in a realm of relativity. It is not absolute truth, or perfect truth, but it is the truth for us. For instance, if somebody hits me on the head with a stick, I cannot say that this is unreal because in fact the bamboo strikes me and I feel the pain. It is a sort of reality and one cannot deny it; it is one tier of truth—a superficial or relative truth. The question is, where, in which realm is this regarded as truth? The answer is, within the realm of our thought process. For our deluded and diluted thinking process, this misery in which we live is truth.

The other tier is the absolute truth beyond which there is nothing. It is the Oneness, the That-ness.

We are now situated between the two tiers. Our whole life is conditioned by this realm of relative truth, whereas in the state of the Absolute, the Ultimate, everything is unconditioned. The transformation from relative truth into absolute truth cannot be a planned process. But people are so dependent on timetables that scheduled processes are regarded as indispensable.

At the present stage our mind is very conditioned. Therefore, when we try to put its individual force—the totality of attention—on our mental picture, it often happens that we either distort the picture by our thoughts, or we distort the mental force by our thinking processes. This is all due to the scattered condition of the mind. It takes time to distinguish between meditative attention and ordinary thought. The latter can be used when thinking seriously of an image that has been placed in front of us. That is a normal thinking process. But putting the attention on the picture of the image projected in the mind is a part of meditation.

What qualities the mind should have has always been considered an important question and it is here that many people make mistakes. Many would-be meditators, due to the lack of these qualities, waste their time and, going in the wrong direction with their meditation, achieve nothing. It is for this reason that many ancient *āchārya*s denied the importance of meditation, because, according to them, the denial of meditation is meditation and its acceptance is delusion. This is a very subtle point. However, other *āchārya*s lay down guidelines for meditation, such as that the mind should be clear, attentive and focused on one point without distortion or disturbance.

When we try to bring this about, we discover how mischievous the mind is, how scattered it is and how unable it is to give itself in totality. It is so active that it wants to do a hundred different things at the same time; its energy or force is so divided that nothing is seen as it is in reality. Indeed so constantly and rapidly does it move that everything perceived by it is a delusion. We cannot see anything clearly or perceive one single thing that is undistorted. It is like sitting in a fast-moving car or train. We are not able to see anything outside clearly and it seems that the trees and electricity poles are shooting past us. But we know, of course, that this is an illusion; it is not the objects that are shooting by, it is we who are moving so fast.

We fail to perceive the nature of That-ness because of the unstable state of our mind. The mind must first be pacified and in order to do this, we meditate. By meditating on one object, we wean our mind away from constant movement to steadiness. Steadiness of mind is, of course, also a state, but we have to accept that state for the time being. An *āchārya* explained the matter thus: 'If you have a piece of paper which has always been rolled up in one direction and you want to straighten it out, you will have to roll it in the opposite direction.'

It is dangerous to put the mind into a state of dullness. Some people think that if they immerse themselves in an object and slide into a sort of doze, that is meditation, and because their mind is no longer scattered they think that they have stabilised it. But one does not stabilise one's mind by letting it get absorbed in this manner; on the contrary, it is the wrong approach to meditation because clarity and attentiveness of mind are lost in this practice. Sometimes, by sinking into this sort of drowsiness, after a period, people may achieve a kind of peacefulness or a pleasurable feeling of physical and mental well-being and relaxation. And if this state is maintained for a longer period, the breathing may even stop for some time and they may even think that they have reached the state of *samādhi*, but that is not so. If people are in such a doze that the attentiveness, alertness, active participation and clarity of mind are lost, concentration has no meaning or value. Moreover, the positive qualities of mind will be lost and it will become forgetful, inactive and lazy. We must, therefore, take every precaution, right from the beginning, that concentration on the object is accompanied by attentiveness, alertness, clarity and the active force of a participating mind. When it is left unguarded, the mind behaves like a monkey. It never rests on one point, but constantly moves hither and thither. When the mind is steadied by concentration on one object this activity begins to subside. It is important that the energy of the mind should be channelled and directed to one object. During the process of concentration the mind should not be lost or scattered, but watched to see that it does not move in different directions.

It may appear as if the mind is divided anyway, because one part is engaged in making a picture while another part is concentrating on that picture. How, then, is it possible to concentrate with an undivided mind? These apparent contradictions that come up when we discuss meditation are the result of using words to explain metaphysical forces. Each one will have to experiment and find out for himself how to resolve the apparent contradictions. If he is serious, the solution will come by itself.

As stated before, as soon as a mental picture is built the work of thought is finished. When you withdraw the thought you will find that you are losing the picture because the picture was not held by the entire mind; it was held only by your thought. When, for instance, you have built a mental picture of the Buddha you should sustain it with the strength of the fully concentrated mind. You should not treat it as imagination, because it is not a thought. As a matter of fact, you will not even see it as a picture or think of the Buddha at all. The word 'Buddha' is not in your head because there is no memory and thus you cannot remember that name. You just keep the picture in your mind. Hold it without thought, recognition or words. Similarly, if you have made a picture of a globe of light in your mind, you should not think, 'this is a round light', you should have no thoughts, words, or even a memory of the word 'light'. Once you are able to do this—to make and hold a picture in your mind—you will have achieved concentration. And after this has become a fact for you, you will have a great liking and inclination to meditate and you will not ever want to give it up.

When we look at a picture, it is reflected in the eyes; one might say that the picture is seen inwardly through the eyes. The eyes perceive the totality of the picture and not its symbol. Then thought intervenes and identifies the picture as a mountain, painted by a well-known artist, and perhaps urges you to buy it. But the eye itself has no discrimination; it only sees the picture. The sensual mind always distorts outer objects and that is exactly what happens during our attempts to concentrate. We build a picture through the force of thought. Then we put our whole attention on it without thought, or any other disturbing element. After this has been done we hold the picture through the full concentration of an undivided mind. Everything else is pushed away. This is difficult, and we shall have to try it again and again, but later we may find that all of a sudden, perhaps only for a second or so, we are able to focus properly before the mind is scattered again.

We have examined how to acquire the power of concentration necessary for meditation. Now we shall go a step further and find out how to employ, or call upon, our total mind whenever we wish. The average person's mind is weak, but the nature of mind itself is not weak. The Buddha consciousness and the consciousness of the smallest insect are, in essence, not different; mind is mind and its nature is very clear. But the Buddha was able to employ the totality of his mind whenever he wished to do so; in other words, he had full command over his whole mind or consciousness, whereas insects and even ordinary people have not. As a matter of fact, most human beings use only a very insignificant part of their mind; the rest is unused. But the nature of our mind is not weak because it is potentially capable of achieving Buddhahood, which is the highest consciousness man can reach on earth. The purpose of meditation is to train the mind by controlling it and thus bringing it under command.

Most of us are controlled by our mind or, to be exact, by a part of our fragmented and diluted mind. So, from the very beginning, our meditation must begin to control the mind by focusing its total attention on one point. When we have achieved perfection here, we can change our object of concentration and branch out with our meditative practices over a wider field.

Breathing should be normal during concentration. To make it so, Buddhist meditators often use the method of breathing in and out, nine times, in the following manner:

- Breathe in through the left nostril, keeping the right nostril closed; breathe out through the right nostril, keeping the left nostril closed. Repeat this three times.
- Breathe normally through both nostrils three times.
- Now breathe in through the right nostril keeping the left nostril closed; breathe out through the left nostril keeping the right nostril closed. Repeat this also three times.
- Steps one, two and three form one exercise and should be repeated nine times. After step three, step two can be repeated, then steps one, two and three again, and so on. You may continue with this exercise until your breathing is normal.

These breathing exercises are also very helpful in clearing a blocked nose due to a cold. Here is another method used by many yogis to clear a blockage in the nose. If the blockage is in the left nostril, put something hard under the right armpit and keep it there for a few minutes until the nose is unblocked. Similarly, if the blockage is in the right nostril, the hard object should be pressed under the left armpit. The back of a chair may be used for this purpose. It is important that the nose is free from blockages, for these obstructions disturb the practice of meditation very much. Breathing through the mouth is not good and is not recommended for meditation. Great care should be taken that your health is good if you want to practise meditation.

Questions And Answers

Q. *What is the role of will-power in meditation? Is it helpful?*

A. A certain amount of will-power is necessary for everything one wishes to do, including meditation. But will-power alone cannot do the work for you. You cannot achieve concentration without continuous practice.

Q. *Can there be perception of a statue of the Buddha without a movement of thought—pure perception involving just the eye and the statue?*

A. Yes.

Q. *But there is no statue—just a picture in the mind.*

A. Exactly.

Q. *Then, I feel, the analogy is not exact if one says there is only the eye and the picture, because the picture itself is thought. It may not be movement of thought, but it is thought. The picture is created by thought, whereas the statue is not created by thought, except indirectly.*

A. We cannot concentrate our whole mind on an outer

object and so we create a mental picture. After the creation of this mental picture the movement of thought ceases. Now, in the ordinary process, once the movement of thought ceases the picture also disappears because the picture is thought, however, when we focus on the picture through meditative concentration, with the fullness of our mind, it involves the totality of the mind, and this is not of the nature of thought; it is the clarity of the mind which holds the picture. In other words, when we are able to hold a picture with the totality of our mind, the picture is not thought; it is mind. The mind is not thought at that moment.

Q. *But does the mind need a picture?*

A. In deep meditation, the mind can concentrate on mind. But most people need a picture in order to help focus the mind. The picture, created by thought, becomes a sort of invitation to the mind to focus, and when the mind focuses intently the thought disappears in the totality of the mind. But the effect of the thought still remains and that is what the mind holds on to in order not to get scattered. You will find at a later stage that that mental picture has become a reality and the concentration of mind has become a perception.

Q. *Is the memory stored in the brain or in the mind?*

A. I do not know what the scientific answer is to this question: Buddhist literature does not speak about the brain, but only about the organ of the mind.

Whatever our experiences may be, they leave an impression on the basic continuity of mind which, in turn, depends on the duration of the organ. So if the organ undergoes change the continuity is lost. Still, some impressions received in it are very deep and they are the impressions which people sometimes remember in their next life.

Q. *Do clothes have an influence on meditation?*

A. Yes. Always wear loose, comfortable clothing because tight clothing pressing on the body creates tension.

4

OBSTACLES TO CONCENTRATION AND PREVENTIVE MEASURES

We have already discussed the elementary stages in concentration—how to project the picture of an object in the mind and how to concentrate on that picture with the totality of the mind. We shall continue with the same subject, touching especially on the following points:

- The obstacles the beginner encounters when he starts to concentrate.
- How these obstacles present themselves.
- How to proceed further in the direction of the goal which is the achievement of *śamatha.*

We mentioned that concentration should be practised with a totally one-pointed mind; in other words, with great clarity and the full force of the mind. 'Clarity' does not refer to the clearness of the picture which the beginner must project in his mind. At first, the picture may be vague or unstable and the meditator should not spend too much time in making it clear, as this is not required at this stage. But, still, he must use it as a point to concentrate on. However, the mind itself must be absolutely clear, without any haziness or clouding, for it is only in such state of clarity of mind that the object can be reflected. If this state of clarity is combined with the full force of a one-pointed mind directed towards one object only, energy will be created to hold that object. Even one second of laziness or wavering in this process means loss of energy. The real problem, however, is that as soon as the beginner is able to concentrate on an object with the necessary quality of mind, he finds it impossible to meditate, and it is precisely at this stage that he may be disappointed and give up, believing that it is impossible for him to meditate. But in fact, it is not impossible, and the serious meditator should persevere.

There are two types of impediments which present themselves. The first is distraction of the mind. The mind revolts because it does not want to be disciplined and concentrated on one object. Besides, it is obstructed by many thoughts, for it is in its nature to be so distracted. In the beginning this scattering of the mind is the main problem. Later on another impediment appears: the mind loses its clarity and energy. This is because it sinks into the object of concentration. The technical Sanskrit expression for this condition is *nimagnatā,* which means 'going down'. This is a rather dangerous condition because many beginners mistakenly feel that the mind is now becoming steady and so they go on with this harmful practice.

Distraction of the mind is easily recognised, but it is difficult to recognise the sinking of the mind because the difference between this condition and real meditation is a subtle one. So here the meditator must be vigilant. Precautionary measures must be taken right at the beginning, and this is where the will-power must be used—the will-power to keep alert and to watch carefully the concentration of the mind. It is actually not so much watching the trend of concentration (because that can easily become another distraction of the mind); it is more a standing by and keeping ready to observe the emergence of disturbances.

It is advisable to take the two following preventive measures. The first one is *smṛti* or recollection and the other is *samprajñāta* or recognition. *Samprajñāta* implies knowing or recognising the disturbance. This is how it works. First, before going into concentration, draw on your power of recollectedness so that it will be ready to alert you as soon as thought enters the mind. This is very important, because if one is concentrating, and the mind is one-pointedly directed towards either the object or the picture of that object in one's mind, and if, at that moment, thought enters the mind, it is extremely difficult to get hold of. Usually, the meditator becomes aware of thoughts in his mind long after they have entered. This means some weakness in the power of recollection, which should work the instant, thought penetrates the mind. In the beginning, a thought entering the mind is easily recognised because one notices that the mental picture of the object has disappeared; concentration, then, is finished and one must start again. At a later stage, after the aspirant has been practising steadily, the problem becomes rather more difficult because thought will then creep in cunningly like a thief and, without disturbing the picture in the meditator's mind, will go to work on many things. In the meantime, the meditator is still 'concentrating' and holding the picture with the major part of his mind. The problem now is clearly far more difficult to recognise or prevent for the recollection is still not sufficiently strong to warn the meditator. Therefore, at this second stage, when the meditator is a little more advanced, the task of revitalising the recollective faculty becomes very important.

It is interesting to note that in the very beginning it is not too difficult to concentrate; and much later also, when *śamatha* has been achieved, all problems automatically come to an end. The difficulties appear only when the meditator is partly advanced, and so it is during the middle stages particularly that necessary care and precautions should be taken.

A number of months will pass before the beginner has learned sufficiently from his teacher or from books to begin the necessary preparations. And, again, time will pass before he has finished his preparations and decided on the object of concentration. Then, when he starts to concentrate, he will find that he does not get anywhere at all for about two weeks. Perhaps he will achieve some sort of concentration for a few seconds only. Again, when he goes on, he will feel that during his attempts to concentrate the number of thoughts flitting through his mind has increased greatly. Indeed, they seem to increase ever far beyond the number which existed in his mind before he started to concentrate. 'What is wrong with me?' he may ask. 'I had a calm mind before I started my concentration, but now it is turbulent with thoughts.' But in reality this is not so. The fact is that a person who does not meditate never realises how many thoughts arise in his mind. As soon as he starts to concentrate, every thought is recognised, being highlighted.

Through concentration, then, the aspirant becomes aware of the great number of thoughts that pass in and out of his mind, and this is where the real struggle starts. As soon as he has made a picture in his mind of his chosen object, thought will come in and scatter it; then he will set the picture up again only to lose it almost immediately as soon as another thought arises; so it goes on. It is at this stage that an instructor is needed to guide the meditator. It may also happen that the beginner becomes overzealous in trying to keep his powers of recollection and recognition alert, or he may become too intent on his concentration. If this happens he will also lose the faculties of recollection and recognition. Therefore a well-balanced application of all these faculties—concentration, recollection and recognition—is absolutely necessary.

One might compare this problem of adjustment to walking a tightrope. Only a well-trained person can walk the rope and he does so with an umbrella in one hand in order to keep his balance. Similarly, the beginner in meditation should concentrate his attention on the picture in his mind (the rope) while he balances himself with the umbrella of recollection and recognition, so that as soon as a thought enters his mind, he will know it, immediately recollect himself and, without even changing his posture or attention, will discard it and continue his concentration with one-pointedness of mind. Here the meditator can use his will-power by forcefully rejecting stray thoughts entering his mind and directing all his mental energy towards the picture of the object. But, at the same time, he will have to watch carefully whether he has regained the same clear and forceful concentration he had before the thought entered his mind. It could even be that he has improved the picture and that is good, but the main thing to watch out for is that the quality of clarity and forcefulness of concentration have not decreased. This 'watching' should not be done during the process of concentration, but just before or after it.

After the meditator has pushed away stray thoughts and recovered his concentration a number of times, he will need a break of about five to ten minutes. He should have a cup of tea, or wash his face, or go out for a short while, after which he can return to his exercise. If he does not feel too well after the break, he should not continue the exercise until he is quite fit again. After a while, when his concentration begins to steady, the time could be gradually increased so that good progress can be maintained.

As he continues his practice of concentration, the meditator will pass through two distinct phases. One phase, as we have seen, will give him the feeling of an enormous increase of thought; during the second, he experiences a break in the continuity of thought for shorter or longer periods. He will, therefore, at times feel that he has to cope with many thoughts, while the next moment there are no thoughts at all for half an hour or so. Then, after this silent period, thought activity comes back again with full force. This means that the aspirant has entered the second stage on the road to meditation, and it is because of this fluctuation in the number of thoughts that he sometimes has a good period of concentration and at other times, when thoughts are numerous again, a bad one. It is now that he should increase his efforts. In order to stabilise the fluctuation of thought he should increase the time of his concentration. If, for instance, he had been meditating four times a day, he could now prolong the periods and increase the number of times he sits for concentration. When he has done this for a while, he will notice that when thoughts come during his concentration they will disappear again without much effort on his part. At the same time, he will also feel that he has developed some steadiness in holding the picture of the object in his mind. It is precisely at this point that the 'sinking' of the mind can start.

The 'sinking' of the mind is a rather dangerous state because, first, it is very difficult for the meditator, who has the full force of his mind turned on his concentration, to detect it, and secondly, recognition of this state comes only by experience, as it cannot be expressed in words or demonstrated. Only an experienced meditator knows when it happens, because he knows the difference between this and full concentration. The aspirant should revitalise his powers of recollection and recognition and carefully watch the trend of his concentration. He can, of course, smoothly continue his concentration exercises but that may run him into trouble. It is much better at this point if he breaks his concentration deliberately and examines whether his mind is still active and alert, or whether it has started to sink slowly into the object. The 'sinking' of the mind gives a very pleasurable feeling, and many meditators do not want to disturb this feeling of bliss and calmness. Besides this, the mind, although still concentrating on the picture, has yet imperceptibly lost its energy and clarity and has become dull like stagnant water with scum on it. If the meditator continues with his exercise during this particular condition of mind he will find that, after his concentration is finished, his body also carries this sinking feeling and then he just wants to sit idle and relaxed.

Many people like this sort of feeling, but it is not the real *samādhi*, nor will it ever lead to that state. Therefore, however blissful and pleasant the experience may be, the meditator must struggle out of it and get on with real meditation. The difference between real meditation and the state of the sinking mind may perhaps be explained as follows, say that the object of concentration is a cup and the mind a hand. The hand can hold the cup either very loosely, or firmly with full support of the fingers. In the sutras we find the analogy of a man walking along a rough road, holding a cup full of water in his hand. He does not want to spill any of the water and so he must watch the road as well as the cup. In *the* same way, the aspirant has to watch his mind to see that it does not scatter while he concentrates. He also has to watch the picture of the object in his mind. Now the difference between the condition of a sunken mind and meditation lies in the strength with which the mind holds the picture of the object. When the mind is clear and holds the picture with its full force that is all right. But if it becomes a little slack it may lead the meditator to *nimagnatā,* the 'sinking' condition.

Distraction of mind is much easier to watch for and get rid of because when thought comes in and concentration is scattered, the powers of recollection and recognition automatically begin their work. But in the sinking mind it is far more difficult because the mind has not lost the picture, therefore the power of recollection does not come into action, so the meditator goes deeper and deeper into this mentally sunken state, and the longer it continues the more difficult it will be to come out of it. But once the aspirant has experienced the difference between the sinking of the mind and meditation, he should vitalise the powers of recollection and recognition with a greater vigilance than ever before. Then, as soon as the downward trend and the dullness of the mind start, the power of recollection will give the alarm and the power of recognition will break the concentration. The meditator then realises that, as he is still holding the picture in his mind, his concentration must have been broken by his powers of recollection and recognition, and that therefore he must have slipped into the wrong sort of meditation. So he will start again by vitalising his powers of recollection and recognition, recollect his mind and start his concentration again, if possible. But if he has any difficulty in restarting, he should take a short break, go out for a little while, after which he can come back to restart his concentration.

After the meditator has been exercising his power of concentration for a while and the condition of distraction and the sinking problem of the mind have lessened, his period of proper concentration will increase, sometimes even go up to ten or fifteen minutes. The meditator will not feel so tired and he will be able to slowly improve his meditation and make progress to a certain stage without the constant help of a teacher or friend. But if after a few months he is still troubled by distraction and 'sinking', there are certain techniques which he should adopt. These techniques should not be used at the beginning but after the meditator has passed at least the first three stages of progressive concentration, namely:

- The stage where the quantum of thoughts seem to increase tremendously.
- The stage where he experiences a break in the continuity of thought; that is to say, he sometimes has to cope with many thoughts and sometimes there are no thoughts at all.
- The stage at which the rate of disturbance has come down to a lower level and the time of real concentration has increased.

Now at this point the more obvious stages of distraction and sinking of the mind may be replaced by more subtle versions of these two conditions and the meditator's efforts may be hampered by them. He may counteract them in the following manner. If, for instance, the disturbance is a subtle version of distraction, the meditator should darken the room. He should then lower the height of the object he is concentrating on. Similarly, if the aspirant is disturbed by a subtle version of the sinking mind, he should not only increase the light as much as possible but he should also raise the object to a higher level. Another helpful practice for the meditator who is troubled by this sinking condition of the mind is, whenever he goes out, to direct his eyes towards a distant place or point.

If the meditator has progressed to the fourth and fifth stage, all disturbances will have decreased and he will be able to concentrate on an object for about twenty minutes at a stretch without experiencing the slightest disturbance.

This is the beginning of the achievement of steadiness of mind. At this point, the vitalising of the power of recollection and recognition, as well as the condition of alertness of the mind, should be decreased, because at this advanced stage those qualities will not be helpful in prolonging the period of concentration. As the effects of outer disturbances on progressively better concentration decrease, the recollection, recognition and alertness of mind can become disturbing factors. These precautionary measures are necessary and helpful at the beginning of concentration when one has to not only vitalise the powers of recollection and recognition, but also keep the mind alert to combat distraction and thought processes. So while it is not good to be casual in the early stages, alertness is not good at the more advanced stages. Therefore, from the fourth or fifth stage onwards, the meditator should ease off, little by little, the vigorous vigilance and alertness of recollection, recognition and mind. As soon as these faculties of alertness are decreased, the power of undisturbed concentration will automatically increase.

A periodical examination of concentration should always be carried out. This means that, occasionally, after a long period of concentration, the meditator should break the concentration and reflect on its clarity, strength, whether there was any disturbance, and so on. If he finds that all was well, then he can go on with it. If, however, he finds that something was not quite in order he should start again and try to rectify whatever was wrong. Patience, determination to continue and prolong the practice, and being in no hurry to obtain results, are the essential requirements for progress in meditation. The tendency at this stage is for the meditator to become somewhat overconfident. He thinks that since he can now concentrate for half an hour without any disturbance he will go on to meditate for a full hour. This sort of thinking creates another kind of disturbance. The meditator should be content to progress slowly. His time of concentration should be increased only by one or two minutes a week and any sense of hurry or impatience must be put aside.

As time passes, the meditator may find that he is able to maintain sustained concentration for a whole week or so. Then it may suddenly happen that for another week his concentration becomes very disturbed. When this happens, he should look into the condition of his health, or his diet, or his environment. If he has advanced this far in concentration, all these factors are relevant. Eating too much, or sleeping too much, or having too much light in his room may cause the meditator to lose whatever progress he has made and his long-sustained efforts will be nullified. It is therefore absolutely necessary, from this stage of his progress onwards, that he should keep steadily to a strict routine, eat moderately, and keep himself in good health until he has achieved greater control over his concentration and meditation. Once he has achieved this—that is to say he can concentrate without failure for half an hour or so at a time—the meditator can prolong his practice to a much longer period. If that goes well for some time, he is ready for the next step.

The next step to be taken by the meditator is to break the routine. This means, for example, that when he is able to concentrate in the morning for a considerable time and then again in the afternoon, and both periods of concentration are going really well, he gives up meditating the next morning or afternoon as the case may be, and either goes out to do some ordinary work or allows himself to be caught up in some other distracting influence. This, of course, is all by way of a test to find out how it affects him. Therefore the next day, when he starts his concentration again, he must watch carefully whether his peace of mind and control over his power of concentration is as steady and clear as it was before he exposed himself to these outside influences. Again, after he has been practising these variations in routine for some time, he can increase their duration for up to two or three days. These exercises are necessary because the meditator has been living up to this stage in almost complete isolation. He was sealed off from ordinary life, with all its influences, in order to achieve proper concentration and meditation. But now, that he has, to some degree achieved this target, he should slowly ease back again into normal life.

Even a person living in a lonely corner may be engaged in various pursuits, but the purpose of meditation is to prepare an individual by self-purification to live in the midst of the bustle of the world, without being influenced or tainted by it. Exposure to the outer world, then, should be gradual so that the meditator can check carefully whether he is capable of maintaining his grip on concentration. If he finds that, at a certain stage, he is affected by the world he must go back again for a while to the routine of daily meditation. This routine should be exposed more and more to disturbances, including diet and environment. Finally, the meditator must learn to intermingle his concentration with the daily activities of his ordinary life. This means that he must practise concentration while moving around or walking in the street where he has to be careful of the traffic. He must practise concentration while cooking, eating, sleeping, working and so on. In all these practices he must keep a clear picture in his mind of the object he habitually uses for his concentration.

It is recommended that, after one has been meditating for a long period on a certain object and has achieved considerable powers of attention and concentration, one changes the object completely. For instance, if one has been concentrating on a symbol it would be good to change over to sound, or movement, or the body. It is not necessary to concentrate on the new object for long periods of time; one just needs to have a change for a little while. Then one should go back to the original object of one's choice and concentrate on that again for a few days, watching carefully whether this creates any disturbance. If all is well, one should again change to another object.

One should now gradually increase the period of one's

'sitting for concentration'. For example, if one has been sitting for half an hour one should increase it to thirty-five minutes and then, after a week, to forty minutes and so on. In this way the period of concentration should be gradually increased. The *Śāstras* do not speak about hours; they mention 'a quarter of a day' as the time limit for intensive concentration. We may take this to mean three hours. Indeed, according to the scriptures, this is the maximum period allowed for a meditator who has not yet achieved *śamatha*. When that happens there will be no limit to the period of concentration and meditation, because then meditation will become a part of life and it will no longer require a special effort.

Sitting for concentration for three hours at a stretch demands a great deal of effort in the beginning. The meditator must firmly imprint on his mind:

- I am going to meditate on this particular object and my faculties of recollection and recognition will be standing by, ready to intervene as soon as any disturbance comes into my mind, so that I will recognise and remedy that condition immediately.
- I shall go on meditating for three hours without a break if disturbance does not present itself.

These two disciplines (which the meditator can repeat as often as necessary) call for a great deal of effort at the beginning. If, however, there are no disturbances and everything proceeds smoothly, then, after three hours the concentration will involuntarily break and the meditator will know that he is at the end of the time which he mentally set for himself at the beginning. Now he must review his whole effort over these three hours and see whether everything went all right, or perhaps something could be improved. Even if the three hours of concentration is perfect, the meditator cannot assure himself that he will achieve *śamatha* soon within a certain time. The achievement of *śamatha* depends on many things, such as the meditator's temperament. It does not matter whether some periods of meditation are short and others long; what is important is that one's daily meditation should be maintained at all costs. (Naturally, if one has the time, daily meditation for three hours is recommended.) One must try to avoid too many gaps between the sessions. If one has to go without meditation on one day, it will be necessary to pick it up again the next day. One must just continue with this practice and wait patiently until *śamatha* comes.

A meditator who has advanced to this stage has already developed considerable control over his thoughts and powers of discrimination. He entertains whatever thought he wishes, and puts aside all else. This in itself is very useful for a person even though he has not yet achieved *śamatha*. From this time onwards, the meditator must put forth his efforts towards making his mental picture of the object as clear as possible. As I said before, it is not necessary for the would-be meditator to achieve a clear picture at the beginning; it does not really matter whether his picture is hazy or unsteady. But now that he has advanced to the stage where he can meditate for three hours at a time he must try to make his mental picture as clear as possible. With full control over thought and with discrimination, he should from now on try to improve it until every detail of the picture is as clearly outlined as the original object. This exercise is of great importance for a later stage when the meditator has achieved *śamatha* and is ready to go into higher meditation.

Questions And Answers

Q. *How often should one meditate and at what times?*

A. If you take your meditation seriously it is recommended that you practise four times a day namely, early in the morning before sunrise, later in the morning before noon, in the afternoon before sunset, and at night before midnight. For casual meditators, to meditate once a day, preferably early in the morning before sunrise, is sufficient. Unlike other systems, Buddhists do not recommend meditation at the times of sunrise, midday or noon, sunset and midnight.

Q. *You mentioned that the powers of recollection and recognition have to be kept on the alert, so that as soon as a thought enters the mind during concentration they warn the meditator and get rid of the thought. Would these two powers which are constantly kept on the alert not create a disturbing tension in the mind?*

A. I said that at the beginning, before concentration begins, the powers of recollection and recognition should be vitalised so that if any stray thought enters during the process of concentration, recollection will sound the alarm and recognition will get rid of the thought. But one cannot keep the powers of recollection and recognition active during the process of concentration because this would also be a process of thought. These powers are vitalised at the beginning and stand on the alert ready to function whenever necessary; that is to say, as soon as any disturbance enters the mind during the process of concentration. Then, and then only, will these faculties involuntarily enter and warn the meditator against the intruder.

Q. *Will those people who have achieved the power to concentrate for hours at a time attain the powers known as the* siddhis?

A. A person who has advanced so far as to meditate for three hours at a time is certainly no longer an 'ordinary' person. But the *siddhi*s will only come after *śamatha* has been achieved and the mind is absolutely quiet.

Q. *Could you please tell me what* śamatha *actually is?*

A. *Śamatha* is the name for a state of mind which is achieved after learning to concentrate for a long period, up to three hours. This practice of intense concentration develops some sort of energy in the body which then becomes very light and easy to handle. Later, this same energy goes also to the mind giving it a very happy feeling. This feeling is not a sign that one has reached *samādhi* or nirvana—it is just a happy feeling. This psychophysical feeling remains for a while, but as one goes on with the practice of concentration, it will lessen and one will then get the power to concentrate for as long as one wishes, whether it be seven days, ten days or a month, without any disturbance. At the same time one will achieve the combined equanimity of body and mind. So after having done all these practices and after having obtained stability of body and mind, one will finally reach *śamatha* and then one can meditate for years and years because the mind will then strictly obey the meditator's wishes. That state, that stability of mind, is *śamatha.*

Q. *How can a man born blind concentrate on an object?*

A. A blind man can concentrate on sound or shape. But, of course, handicapped people will have to put more effort into their meditation because their handicap will also be an impediment in this particular field.

Q. *Would it not be easier for a blind man to concentrate because he is not distracted by sight?*

A. I do not know, but I do not think so. A person who is born blind may be disturbed in a much more concentrated way by his remaining four senses. He must experiment and find out what is the best way for him.

5

PROGRESS OF MEDITATION: ONE-POINTEDNESS, WISDOM AND INSIGHT

If a person continues with his practice of concentration certain changes will take place in his body and, later on, in his mind also. These changes will come about quickly and easily in the case of some meditators, while in others they will appear only after much effort and practice. This is so because they depend on many factors such as the meditator's background, his karma, the quality of his practice, and so forth. But any person who continually practises concentration and who does not make any basic mistakes ought to achieve good results sooner or later.

This change is first noticed in the body because the superficial mind used by ordinary people, which is inclined to be *sthūla* or gross, depends for its function on the body.

The subtle mind, however, does not depend on the body at all. Beginners meditate with the gross mind, and the subtle mind does not function in the early stages of meditation. However, as the aspirant gains control over his gross mind and brings it to a standstill through continual practice in one-pointed concentration on a particular object, he creates a change in his body. This is because when the mind is one-pointed, the flow of the vital airs in the body is brought under control. In the ordinary state, when the mind is scattered, the vital airs which carry the subtle forces are in disorder and this affects not only the body but the mind as well. Therefore, by controlling the mind, the body is also brought into a state of harmony. When the meditator reaches this stage, he feels a pleasant sensation throughout his body. This pleasant feeling, or lightness, which enables the meditator to handle his body with much greater ease, is often mistaken as an achievement and people frequently stop here, wallowing in this pleasant feeling. This may lead to the meditator losing everything that he gained with so much effort. The feeling of lightness in the body is a sign that a certain progress has been made and that one is coming near to the achievement of real meditation; it is not a result in itself. Therefore, when the meditator feels his body growing lighter he should not allow his mind to be scattered. On the contrary, he should intensify his one-pointed concentration, meditation and recollectedness. Then, after about a week, the pleasant feeling in his body will settle down. He may feel that it is decreasing but in fact it is not. He is gaining control over the situation and therefore his mind is not disturbed by his feelings.

Almost directly following on this pleasant bodily feeling comes an indescribable feeling of contentment and happiness in the mind. This feeling does not come during meditation but after it. This sensation creates another problem because once more the meditator is inclined to hold on to it. But he must be firm and break off his meditation at the proper time and have some leisure when he can go out for a walk, talk to people, listen to music, and so on. In this way, he will prevent himself from 'drowning' in meditation in order to experience the after-effects of contentment. When he is firm with himself, this feeling of happiness of mind will also settle down.

One can clearly see that the pleasant feeling of the body combined with the sense of happiness in the mind together form a yoke. In Sanskrit, yoga means a harmonious combination of two things, which in this case are the body and mind. Concentration under such conditions is called *śamatha* because all disorderly functions and scattering of mind have now been pacified and eliminated.

When the mind and body are thus in harmony and the meditator directs his mind on to a material object for concentration, he will experience a sort of *samādhi*. At present, we do not have the equanimity of mind necessary to concentrate on objects exactly as they are, because our mind is always active and therefore constantly distorts things.

Perhaps without having achieved *samādhi* there is no way of perceiving anything as it is in reality.

The first part of the word, *sama* in *samādhi* denotes equality. 'Equality' means, in this case, that the content of the object and that of the mind should be equal. 'Equality' and 'harmony' can exist even between a pot and its lid at the place of union, but if the lid does not fit the pot exactly there is neither equality nor harmony between them. Similarly, there should also be equality between the known and the knower, or the mind. But at present, due to the way in which the mind works, there is disorder in that area. For example, the mind works through the eyes. Sight is supposed to perceive the object directly and present it without distortion to the mind. But does it? Is the colour which we perceive, for instance, always exactly correct? And when we look at a round shape which is about a hundred meters away, do we see it in its true size? Distance reduces the clarity of colour and shape and so the object gradually changes according to the distance and the acuteness of our eyesight. So, by the time the image touches the field of our perception we see something different. The same could be said when an object is placed so near to a person that his eyes cannot perceive it properly. Thus, because the mind distorts, there is an inequality between the mind and the object.

When the mind works through the ears the same thing applies. If someone speaks from a great distance, depending on the distance and our ability to hear, we either hear distorted words or only vague sounds. Naturally, different people hear different distortions. However, if the distant speaker comes nearer the reception becomes clearer, and when he is very near there should no longer be any distortion. But if thought comes in when one is in the process of listening, or looking at a distant object, there is a great deal of distortion and a wrong apprehension of the spoken word or perception of the object.

When the state of *śamatha* has been achieved our minds are able to concentrate on the object with great equanimity and perceive it exactly as it is without the least distortion. But this achievement does not mean that we have reached absolute reality or have realised the ultimate truth of the phenomenon. We have to go much further if we want to arrive at that point. But what has been achieved is a power of mind which can concentrate on an object with great equanimity. When *śamatha* has been achieved the meditator can greatly reduce his efforts at concentration, for the danger of scattering of the mind or the slow sinking down of the mind has now been overcome. Also, once the meditator has gone through the process of harmonising his mind and body he need no longer keep his powers of recollectedness and recognition on the alert. This can all be dropped because these disturbances will not occur again. Moreover, he will also find that no inconvenience, such as tiredness of the body, stiffness in the legs, will arise while practising meditation, for the body will have learned to adjust itself and will make no demands to be fed or to be exercised at a certain time. It is now capable of doing any work for any length of time.

The achievement of *śamatha* is indeed a landmark in meditation. We must not forget however that it is not the ultimate goal, but it is the point from which real meditation starts. Until its achievement we are only training our minds to concentrate without being disturbed by thought, or getting into the sinking condition. Eventually, the serious person perseveres with his meditation for the sake of meditation only and enters into the eight types of *samādhi*; that is to say the four types of *rupa samādhi* and the four types of *nirupādhi samādhi*.

It is a real luxury for the meditator to explore these different grades of *samādhi*. But let us not go too far ahead; let us stay with the meditator who has achieved *śamatha* and who is about to explore the first stage of *rupa samādhi*.

The meditator has achieved a harmonious relationship between his body and mind. When he begins to concentrate his mind, his body immediately cooperates. In the beginning, when a person is trying to achieve *samādhi*, thought and discrimination are needed to probe into certain aspects of, for instance, contemplation. Thought is needed to produce a picture of the object he is concentrating on and discrimination is needed to assess whether he is meditating rightly or wrongly, and whether the picture he has made is clear or not. The use of thought and discrimination are thus indispensable for the beginner before he enters *samādhi* and directly after he comes out of it. But when he develops more spiritually and meditates for the pleasure of meditating there are certain higher states to be achieved, all of which are prescribed in the *Śāstras*.

The *Śāstras* mention three different realms. The first is the realm of *kama* which is the ordinary stage in which most people live. The second is that of *rupa* which is the stage of form. The third is the stage of *nirupādhi*, the realm of the formless, or the realm beyond form.

The mind in the stage of *kama* is the ordinary uncontrolled mind. When *samādhi* has been achieved (that is to say the first stage of *rupa samādhi*) the mind has become much more refined and the meditator finds himself in a state of peace. If he has been meditating at this stage for a while he finds that there is no need for thought or discrimination. So he may now eliminate these and develop a *samādhi* without them. When he has achieved this second stage he neither needs thought to get into *samādhi* nor to get out of it. Before *samādhi*, during *samādhi*, and while coming out of it, the meditator remains without thought.

After the cessation of thought, the feeling of happiness that remains in the mind of the meditator becomes a disturbance, for he finds the state of *samādhi* more peaceful without the additional feeling of happiness. Therefore the meditator will set out to eliminate it. The cessation of happiness can be achieved by practising either *śamatha* or *samādhi* and when the meditator has successfully accomplished it, he will find himself in a neutral state which is neither happy nor unhappy. This is the third realm of *rupa samādhi*; it is much higher and much more peaceful than the stage of *śamatha.*

When this mental state of happiness has ceased, the meditator will notice that there remains one more disturbing factor. This is caused by *sukha vedanā* or a pleasurable sensation in the body, which has a disquieting effect on him. So, finally the meditator takes this disturbance also in hand and gets rid of it. When this feeling has also subsided to *upekshā* or a neutral point, where there is neither pleasure nor unpleasantness, the meditator has achieved the fourth and highest stage of *rupa samādhi.*

After this he will feel that the relationship between mind and body is not really helpful to his meditation and he will try, therefore, to make the mind completely independent of the body. In order to achieve this he has to practise the *samādhi.* of bodylessness (*nirupādhi samādhi*). *Nirupādhi samādhi* is also divided into four stages. To begin with, the meditator will have to give up concentrating on any object which has a shape, form, or any other embodiment, and meditate only on unlimited emptiness. This is not the emptiness of *śūnyatā* but the unlimited emptiness of *ākāśa* (space), which the meditator takes as his subject for *samādhi.*

Next, after he has been meditating in this way for a while, he feels that he must no longer concentrate on a subject which seems to be outside himself, and so he focuses his meditation on the limitlessness of consciousness. This means that he is entering the second stage of *nirupādhi samādhi.*

All that is left now of the practice of meditation is concentration; but concentration itself is now a source of disturbance and he has to eliminate it also. This means that the meditator is entering the fourth or highest stage of *nirupādhi samādhi*

It is interesting to note that in order to rise higher and higher in his meditation, the meditator has to gradually eliminate one refined sensation after another and one practice after another. When he has finally emptied himself completely he achieves the fourth stage of *nirupādhi samādhi*. From now on the system of *samādhi* will not work for the meditator because, by eliminating concentration, he relinquished the last active tendency of his mind and therefore he will need to enter into a different type of meditation.

The Buddhist and Hindu teachings about the different stages of *samādhi* are similar. The technical terms may be different but the grading of the stages and the systems of elimination are, with an occasional slight variation, common to all the ancient traditions of Indian meditation. Although, meditational systems may differ in the beginning, they all correspond to each other in the higher stages, especially in the *rupa* and *nirupādhi samādhi* stages.

I have briefly sketched for you, without going into complicated technical points, the progress of meditation in an orderly way, and pointed out what can be expected in the way of disturbances before achieving the higher stages. This is the general pattern up to and including the stages of *śamatha* and *samādhi*. However, in the Buddhist system, a meditator who has achieved the stage of *śamatha* is usually not encouraged to go ahead and luxuriate in the eight stages of the two types of *samādhi*. As soon as *śamatha* has been achieved, the meditator's mental qualifications are held to be sufficient to develop a more spiritual kind of meditation, and they therefore recommend that from the achievement of *śamatha* onwards, the meditator should concentrate his mind on investigating the reality of things for a number of years. As mentioned previously, Buddhists always work with a two-tier system of temporal or relative truth and ultimate or absolute truth. The reality of things is also divided into two tiers, namely that of the relative world and that of the absolute world. So in order to discover the reality of things, or approach the absolute truth, it is recommended that meditation on the Four Noble Truths should be practised. For Buddhists, the ultimate goal to be achieved is nirvana, the state in which all shortcomings of the mind have ceased to exist. The method for the achievement, of nirvana is twofold, namely:

- *Prajñā,* the establishment of right insight, right knowledge or wisdom.
- *Upāya,* the means or the method by which *prajñā* may be established.

When *śamatha* has been achieved, meditation on the Four Noble Truths is recommended and later, on *śūnyatā* or That-ness. These meditations are designed to help root out *avidyā*, or the state of inner misconception and ignorance. Because of ignorance, we live in *samsara*, the ever-changing scenes of life, and it is through perseverance with the practices of these prescribed types of meditation that the serious meditator finds that *śamatha* becomes the method (*upāya*) by which *prajñā* is established. *Prajñā* is the knowledge which knows the Is-ness, the That-ness. It is the Wisdom which knows the Truth.

Every phenomenon which exists in a particular form is misunderstood by 'I', the individual person. The 'I' exists; we cannot deny that. But we can deny the existence of the individual as understood by us at present. The concept of 'I' comes to us through *avidyā*, by which we perceive an entity who has an independent nature of his own (*svabhāva*). But the Buddha said that nothing of this kind exists; everything exists in a field of relativity. If a thing exists—as we think it does—as an independent being, it should be able to know when we analyse it. But everything is not in a position to recognise this. For example, we usually think in the following manner: 'I am' and 'I am here'. We casually think about 'I', but we do not know in which reality the image of 'I' exists. We take 'I' for granted and think that it exists and is not dependent on anything else. But when we begin to investigate the matter further what do we find? We say: I am here and this is my mind, but the mind is not 'I'; this is my name, but the name is not 'I'. And by probing deeper and deeper we learn that there is nothing in particular which can be pointed to as being the 'I'. This is possible because the 'I' is only apparently in coexistence with other phenomena such as the body, the mind, one's name, one's actions and thoughts. Moreover, the 'I' is related to and dependent on all these phenomena. So the 'I' exists in an interdependent way in time, space, thought and so on. On analysing the matter, one finds that while outwardly no 'I' can be pinpointed, there is something of that nature in the realm of interdependence and that this fact is not realised or comprehended by the present, ordinary mind. But when a meditator has achieved the power of concentration (*śamatha*), he can investigate every object or phenomenon with a powerful one-pointedness of mind which enables him to penetrate into absolute reality.

Absolute reality, or Voidness, or That-ness, is called *śūnyatā* in Sanskrit. Even renowned scholars of both ancient and modern times have not understood correctly what Nāgārjuna meant by his exposition of the doctrine of Voidness and they mistakenly interpreted *śūnyatā* as annihilation. However, to establish truth, or even a relative truth, by negation, is quite a different matter. This system is equivalent to reaching the positive through the negative. For instance, there is a pot. We look at it and perceive it in a distorted way, as usual.

What we have to do now is to negate our distorted interpretation—all our conceptions about it—and then, washed clean of our superimposed distortions, the reality of the pot as it is will appear. In a similar way we shall perceive reality when we develop insight and wisdom.

We are always full of thoughts and words because we work through them constantly, and without them we would not be able to do anything at all. For whatever we talk and think about, we make use of images. These images are usually negative and have a distorting effect on our action as well as on our comprehension and perception. Therefore, because we are conditioned, we never see anything as it really is. An untrained person is in no position to perceive accurately or precisely the details of an outer object. Similarly, when one looks into the inner realms it is very difficult to see any phenomenon without distorting it. But as we have mentioned before, for a serious and advanced meditator, insight into the reality of things can be obtained through *prajñā* because it negates all the distorting forces which appertain to the imagination of 'I' and 'mine'. Thus he succeeds in his investigation of phenomena as they really are.

So the meditator in the state of meditation divides phenomena also into two parts: one part contains all that belongs to the 'I' and the 'mine' and the other part all the other things. Thus a division is made between the *pudgala* (which is the individual) and the *dharma* (which is everything else which does not belong to the individual) and then *prajñā* investigates them. It investigates, on the one hand the *pudgala-nairātmya,* or the essence of the centreless-ness of 'I', or egoless-ness, and on the other, *dharma-nairātmya,* or the centreless-ness of all other things, the non-substantiality of things. If the meditator has realised these two truths, he will keep on investigating everything and thus learn to know the Truth. This is not realised, at first by direct knowing, but by inference or *anumāna.* He will discover that things are not as solid, as independent or as unchangeable as they appear to be. In this way the meditator acquires a knowledge or insight into the voidness of the phenomenon. And as he continues with this sort of meditation he comes to a state where he can perceive reality without thought or distortion, with a direct vision of *nairātmya* or *ātmā*-lessness. This is *prajñā,* the wisdom of insight which knows the Truth, or *vipassanā,* the special vision into reality.

Naturally *prajñā* itself can be meditated upon and developed further. When this stage has been achieved, a complete transformation takes place. This means that the whole world of phenomena as perceived hitherto by ignorance and misconception will disappear, and an absolutely new type of seeing and knowing will take its place. Ignorance has given place to wisdom. This is *vipassanā.*

Questions And Answers

Q. *Could you tell us more about* prajñā *and the action of* śūnyatā*?*

A. Things are always in the realm of *śūnyatā,* but we do not see it or realise it. *Prajñā* enables us to look into the nature of things as they exist.

Q. *Can one say that* prajñā *is awareness of emptiness, or that it is the wisdom which is awareness of emptiness?*

A. Yes, but even the word 'emptiness' is difficult to understand in this context because in Buddhism emptiness does not mean non-existence.

Q. *Can one say that wisdom is awareness of emptiness?*

A. Yes.

Q. *And that attributing an independent, changeless existence as the centre of anything is* avidyā*?*

A. Yes, up to the stage of emptiness.

Q. *What is the relationship between* śūnyatā *and* prajñā*?*

A. *Śūnyatā* is the object and *prajñā* is the awareness of the object. *Prajñā* investigates and comes to know the *śūnyatā*, which is the dissolution of the 'I'.

Q. *Are is-ness and awareness synonymous?*

A. No, the is-ness is the object and the awareness is an attribute of consciousness.

Q. *You said that if a person lived a pure life and was sincere, he would achieve a state of harmony and wisdom with or without meditation. Then you described a method by which he might reach nirvana. Is not living a pure life in itself meditation? I realise that living a pure life is not the work of a moment and that it may take a lifetime or even many lifetimes to achieve wisdom and realisation. We need awareness in order to lead a pure life: why, then, do we need a special method to reach this insight? Do we really need a method, such as you described, since awareness of the pure life is itself meditation?*

A. In an interdependent nature, a pure life and meditation go together. I do not think that at the present stage of our development (in which there is a disorderly state of mind) it is possible for us to live a pure life. Naturally, the very effort to try to do so will purify the mind to some extent and this, in turn, will help one to lead a pure life. Purity of life and purity of mind, then, help each other and if we do not meet any obstacles these qualities will increase. It is true that our very awareness of a pure life is a part of the effort to lead it. However, methods and systems of meditation are scheduled to work within a time limit. This means that if a person wants to end this ordinary sort of living as soon as possible—either in this life or, if that is not possible, in other lives—he would have to follow the described methods and systems of meditation and not wait for his natural development, which would take a long time.

Q. Does every person who is training for meditation need a guru?

A. That depends on the person. According to Buddhist training methods, an absolute beginner cannot do without an instructor; every *śrāvaka* needs a guru. But for how long the instructor is needed depends entirely on the progress of the individual pupil. In a few cases, a guru is not needed. A Pratyeka Buddha in the becoming does not need a guru.

6

TOTALITY OF PERCEPTION AND THE FOUR NOBLE TRUTHS

Whatever method is adopted, the goal of meditation should be to achieve a state of mind which is a totality of perception. Buddhists recognise four different types of perception.

First, there is ordinary perception by the sensory mind (*indriya-jñāna*) which comes to us through our eyes, ears, and so on.

Secondly, there is *mano-vijñāna* or inner perception which remains only for a short period of time with an ordinary person, for it is almost immediately disturbed and destroyed by relative or associated thoughts.

The third is *svasamvedanā* which means the perception of the mind or consciousness itself. This is also perceived in the ordinary state.

The fourth is yoga perception which can only be achieved when one has developed one-pointedness of mind through the practice of meditation. After we have achieved the yoga perception, we shall be able to meditate on many phenomena. At present there is no way by which we can perceive *śūnyatā* or *anityata* (the changeableness of compounded things). We know about these things only by inference. In other words, our mind only learns through logic and reason about some facts which we are not able to perceive in any other way. But when a meditator develops one-pointedness of mind and achieves *śamatha,* he will be able to proceed further. Thus after *śamatha* he will achieve *prajñā,* or the wisdom which knows the Truth; then *vipassanā,* or the sight, which will enable him to venture out into the unknown, of which a person in the ordinary state of mind has no conception.

In Buddhism, devotional types of meditation such as *dhyana, samādhi* and *samāpatti,* are not considered important. What is regarded as important is the development of the power of enquiry, discrimination and analysis, and this can only be achieved through *vipassanā* when the mind is in the same concentrated state as in *śamatha.* But in *śamatha* the mind remains concentrated on one point only, while in the state of *vipassanā* it is not centred. On the contrary, it enquires, thinks and analyses without distraction or sinking; it retains its full energy. It is in this state of mind that a person should meditate on the Four Noble Truths—the reality of suffering, the cause of suffering, the cessation of suffering, and the nature of the cessation of suffering.

In his first sermon, the Buddha repeated the Four Noble Truths three times to his five disciples, and in this first message he gave the entire doctrine of Buddhism. He expounded and repeated them in accordance with the mental development of his disciples, explaining them, as it were, step by step. In the first exposition, the Buddha simply numerated the Four Noble Truths saying: This is the truth of suffering, this is the truth of the cause of suffering, this is the cessation of suffering, and this is the way to achieve the cessation of suffering. When his disciples had thought over, meditated on and contemplated this, he gave them further guidance. He said: The truth of suffering must be known, the cause of suffering should be eradicated, the cessation of suffering must be achieved, and the way of the achievement of the cessation of suffering must be practised. Thus he added something to the Truths by not only pointing out the reality of suffering but by declaring that it must be eradicated. The cessation of suffering must therefore be achieved and the way to the achievement of the cessation of suffering must be practised. The disciples meditated again. Then the Buddha gave the third sermon: The truth of suffering must be known, but there is nothing to be known; the cause of suffering must be eradicated, but there is no such cause to be eradicated; the cessation of suffering must be achieved, but there is no such thing to be achieved; the way which leads to the cessation of suffering must be practised, but there is no such way to be practised. This was the culmination of the teaching of the Four Noble Truths.

It is clear from this that the Buddha first made certain statements that pointed to a reality. First he simply stated the subject; then, the 'musts' were added to the initial statements; and, finally, he negated all the statements he had previously made. This indicates to any meditator who begins to experience a transcendental state of mind, the necessity for proceeding gradually. If he follows this hint, he will reach a state where the meditator, the object of meditation and the act of meditation all dissolve into nothingness, into voidness. In short, we could say that whatever is perceived by us in our ordinary state of mind must be dissolved or transformed.

There must be a change. And this change in the present working condition of our mind is the purpose of meditation; it is the beginning of meditation. Once this transformation takes place, there is neither a beginning nor an end because there is no measurement in time. We might call it a realisation of Isness, of things as they are, or the dissolution of the mind into higher state of consciousness.

There is something that troubles me and perhaps troubles all of us. We all have well-developed personalities; we have had a good education; we enjoy taking part in serious discussions about the spiritual life. We think, read, study and enquire into these matters in depth. From time immemorial there have been numerous religious systems, traditions, doctrines, philosophies and schools, yet man is unable to end the suffering of all living beings in general and of his own species in particular. Actually, his suffering seems to have become more acute although he is supposed to have reached the highest level of consciousness and to be evolving in accordance with the theory of evolution. But is that so? Is man's level of consciousness of a high order and is it developing or unfolding to an ever higher state? Experience reveals that it is not developing, but rather deteriorating.

Man has acquired great knowledge in the fields of science, technology and in all temporal, material fields and by it he has provided himself with all that is necessary for living a more comfortable life. But the misery of the mind—the inner body—does not seem to be decreasing. We may discuss subjects of a lofty nature in the fields of philosophy and religion, but our thoughts on philosophical subjects become immaterial and are left high and dry in the face of the stark reality of conflict, contradiction and disorder in the everyday lives of so many people. Even in one single day, whether during the morning or evening, whether we are sleeping, eating or talking, our minds are always in a state of contradiction and conflict between 'I', or my present individual self and 'the others', or society. Having observed all this, one may wonder what is the use of all these great systems, doctrines and philosophies, since we are not able to apply their principles to the upliftment of humanity. The suffering of mankind is not an illusion, it is not *maya* as many like to think; it is a fact—a reality of life which has to be faced by everyone. And we, so-called spiritual people, have become almost helpless under these circumstances, are not only incapable of doing good to the world at large but we are not able to be helpful to even a single individual.

When I was a child, I was placed in a monastery to become a monk—a good person who would benefit a large number of people. But looking back on my life, I cannot think of one person who has become more peaceful or less violent as a result of my talks or of my contact with him. It seems to be that we are not able to do anything for other people; we can only help ourselves. I wonder then whether it is of any use to hope that in the future we shall be able to help with the upliftment of mankind. It may be worth while to consider the following questions:

- Even if we are not able to help the entire community, is there any method by which people could develop through our contact with them and be inspired to live a better or more spiritual kind of life?
- Are we really incapable of benefiting even a single person by bringing about some change in his mind?
- Would it be better to do something about our personal transformation and development first?

Perhaps we could diffuse more loving-kindness or give a message which would make people less violent and the world a happier place to live in. Then mankind might advance towards the discovery and realisation of Truth.

We do many things, but when we seriously examine ourselves at the end of every action, perhaps nothing has resulted from the effort. Let us, for instance, examine what has happened to the effort which was put into this course. A large number of good and mature people have spent a number of hours patiently listening to these talks. I, myself, came here from a distant city and have been struggling with the English language in order to explain certain things to you. But if we look closely at the entire programme it might seem to have been absolutely useless. What I had to say, I have said; and when I set off for Varanasi there will be nothing to carry back with me because nothing has happened and I have achieved nothing. When I talked to you about meditation, I just repeated words that might just as well have been done by a parrot. These words were noted by you in much the same way as words read in the newspaper—'Oh yes, this was said and that happened', and so forth. This is exactly what happens in the course of our entire life; this tendency is visible in all our activities which are too often valueless and useless. To feel about one's way through life, to earn one's livelihood and to talk casually about philosophical or spiritual subjects neither benefits people in general nor any individual in particular. I may be wrong in thinking that there is no hope or sign of encouragement in the present-day world. Mankind is facing serious problems and no one—neither the politicians nor the religious leaders—seem to have a solution for them. They all appear to be busy but people are still suffering.

Is there, then, any possibility of freedom from these difficulties? Can we find a more effective solution for the problems which face us today—the deterioration of moral values, corruption, poverty, disorder and violence? Everywhere people are talking about human misery and seem to be seriously concerned about it; can we not find a solution and change the world?

Among the many people who talk about these problems it seems as if there must be a number who have the necessary will-power and determination to eradicate at least some of them. But perhaps, after all, people are not so seriously concerned with humanity's predicament except when they themselves are personally involved. We talk about violence and wars, but our inner consciousness remains unmoved. We may say, 'It is a bad war,' but we do not have the force of mind even to wish that wars should end unless, as we said, our own lives are endangered. Similarly, we may read in the newspaper that people were killed, but our minds are not moved. We may talk about it, but it is only talk, and we never use our mental force towards the ending of such problems. We may vaguely think about it, but our total mental force is not directed towards ending violence so that in the future mankind will not suffer this kind of immorality.

The Buddha taught us that suffering is a truth. It is a daily truth, because everybody suffers. The cause of suffering will not cease unless we try to find out what it is. There is something lacking in us, and so the question of how to tread the way by which suffering is eradicated never seriously arises.

Serious suffering continues to be present in the world today. Is there anything we can do for humanity in general, or anything we can bring about in our personal, individual self? Can we perhaps think of something which will be immediately effective in bringing about a change for the better?

Questions And Answers

Q. *You said that we are not able to do anything for the majority of people but that we could perhaps do something for ourselves. But you also said that Truth cannot be eliminated, so it must be here even in this dark time of Kali Yuga in which we find ourselves. We have to polish ourselves in order to find it, and in the process we shall very gradually progress. Where there is Truth, there must be progress and no effort is lost. Although we may not make much progress in meditation, surely even meditation at the level where we achieve a certain sense of peace and bliss is valuable in itself.*

A. Of course, people can meditate and can develop and those efforts are not lost. But the question I was trying to put before you is: would it not be possible for us to improve the standard of human society and make it better by our efforts, by our meditations and by leading a pure life? And even if the whole of human society may not benefit by it, at least our immediate surroundings and those people with whom we have direct contact would. The results of such an effort, and the impact it would make on society should, somehow be visible. Perhaps our 'purity' is so insignificant that it does not reflect and radiate an effective force of energy.

If we blame the society for all the wrong things we do, why do we not think about changing it? There are philosophers who say that society cannot be changed. There are others (together with scientists) who believe that a change in a number of individuals would not produce the required impact to change the society, and that only a radical social change should be striven for. When such a change comes, then, they claim, individuals will also change.

Human society, made up as *it* is of individuals, is indeed obviously and visibly deteriorating. Our moral standards, our behaviour and our dealings with one another are on the decline. And when in this disturbed condition we perform wrong actions, we blame the society in which we live. We say: What else can I do? Everybody else is living this sort of life and if I do not do the same how can I survive? The society would throw me out. Besides, if whatever we do should be in the pattern set by the society, we have to tell lies, be dishonest, injure enemies, and so forth.

The object of the spiritual life is not the development of the individual alone. The spiritual development of the individual is for the sake of others, if not for all. Therefore, I ask again, can we not think of some way by which we could effectively and immediately affect, perhaps not the whole world, but at least a very small part that contains the people we are in direct contact with? Can we think of something that would be more effective than the systems of meditation or philosophy?

Q. *Could you explain a little more what is meant by 'the truth of suffering'? We know that there is widespread suffering but it does not really move us. We still continue to be centred in our own little pleasures and preoccupations. If suffering does not present itself to the consciousness as a tremendous fact, then the question of finding its cessation does not arise. The Buddha did not say, 'Look here, this is suffering'; he said, 'This is the truth which you have to know.' This seems to imply something deeper than simply drawing attention to the suffering which we all know because we have all suffered at some time. The Four Truths are fundamental, so there must be a great deal that is implied in each one of them.*

A. The truth of suffering is what I have been trying to put before you. The Buddha and the whole of the Buddhist teaching is contained in them and in nothing else. The Buddha said that the truth of suffering must be known. This is the first Truth and the keynote of this Truth is that we should know it, which implies that we are not aware of it or understand it. Our efforts do not bring about the required results because our consciousness is not deeply touched by this Truth. Until and unless suffering affects a particular person, directly or indirectly, he does not know it. We are not conscious of suffering as a whole, whether it be the suffering of humanity or of other living beings.

Each one of us has an individual body in which we have built for ourselves our own mental forces, our consciousness and thoughts. We have built a shell around all of this and tried to retain within it these forces for our own private use. This means that our individual mind and consciousness is unconnected with the wholeness of all life, with the all-pervading principle of 'Be-ness'. Since our consciousness is thus unconnected with any outside phenomenon, our efforts become limited to ourselves and so we cannot send out the energy or the force required to help others in an appropriate and effective manner. Whatever we do is self-centred and on a very small scale. It is on account of this that I asked whether we could not think of any possible way by which we could expand our thoughts and our visions, find ways and means to make our consciousness aware of suffering. Whether the way is meditation, another kind of practice, determination, will-power or whatever, it must result in making us more deeply concerned with and aware of the suffering of other beings.

The Buddha said: 'You should know suffering', which implies that we do not really know it. We have all kinds of knowledge about suffering but this does not mean that we know the suffering of others. Awareness of suffering is something else. It is to know suffering as the sufferer does: it means experiencing his suffering with our own consciousness, for we have established a direct relation between suffering outside ourselves and our own consciousness. It is only then, when we make an effort to reduce, if not eradicate, the cause of suffering outside ourselves, that it will be effective.

Q. *But there is a problem here. If I know suffering as the sufferer does, if he breaks down and cries, I would also break down and cry, which does not do any good at all. Is this what is meant by knowing the suffering as the sufferer, or is it something else? Would it be correct to say that if one knows the truth of suffering it would bring about a revolution in oneself? If you just know suffering superficially, or as a piece of news, it does not do anything. But if you know the truth of it, since Truth is powerful, it brings about some kind of a revolution within oneself. It creates a tremendous movement, it releases energy. If one sees the truth of suffering there should be a new energy to go further and enquire into its cause.*

A. I did not mean that one has to know the suffering as the sufferer does, and that when he cries one should cry with him. That would be mere sentimentality. The news of an accident which we read in the newspapers has a very different kind of effect in our minds. I read that a plane has crashed in, say, the United States and I know the number of people who died, but the occurrence has no effect on my feelings or my mind. But if the same thing happened in Varanasi while I am there and I read about it in the newspapers, that would disturb me more, especially if the names of the victims were not mentioned, for I would worry about whether friends of mine were involved. There is a difference for me between an accident in America and an accident in Varanasi. The newspapers every day are full of news related to events resulting in the death of people. None of it disturbs us, except that one news item which is connected with ourselves. This shows that our relationship with suffering is not a true one. Who suffers makes a difference for us, which means that there is no equality in our relationship; it is exclusive and personal. Even when you think that you have a truly fine relationship with a particular person, your thoughts really never touch him because he is only an image in your mind, built by your own thought process and having nothing to do with the real person. So, although you may think that you have a great affection for your friend, the truth of the matter is that the affection you feel is not for your friend but for the image of your friend which your thoughts have created in your mind. It is this image-making thought process, constantly going on within our minds which reduces the true meaning of love, for it is evident that one does not love one's friend but one's own self. This phenomenon is even more pronounced where one expects some benefit from another. Real love is quite different. It is an outgoing force which expands and embraces all sentient beings. But we do not know anything about that while we are all the time surrounded by our own images of hatred and love which enclose us in a very narrow shell. Our knowledge of suffering is also only imaginary for it, too, is related to the love of self.

7

FREEDOM FROM MISERY: MORALITY, CONCENTRATION AND WISDOM

Looking at the history of mankind, we see that from time immemorial there have been individuals, or groups of individuals, who have felt the necessity to enquire into life's deeper aspects. As a result of these probings, we have inherited many religious, philosophical and ethical traditions, different in concept and doctrine, which cannot be put together in any orderly way and made to agree with one another. However, if we examine them more closely we find that they have two points in common—one at the beginning and one at the end—and that between these two points there is great variation of religious tradition. For example, all religious traditions concern themselves with freedom from misery; their whole aim and work is to point out a way for the deliverance of all living beings, not just of individuals only.

We find that the entire philosophical tradition of India can be divided into two categories, namely that of the *Ātmāvādins* and the *Anātmāvādins*. The first group accepts the concept of *Ātmā* while the second does not. All philosophical traditions, except Buddhism, can be categorised as that of *Ātmāvādins*; Buddhists are *Anātmāvādins* because they do not accept the concept of *Ātmā* but subscribe to the concept of 'no self', 'no essence of self'. The *Ātmāvādins* say we suffer because we do not realise the nature of *Ātmā*. The Buddhists say that there is no such thing as an independent, unchangeable and permanent *Ātmā* and that there is so much misery in the world because people do not realise this. But I feel that, at our level, to speak about the non-existence of self, or the reality of self, is just a way of expressing oneself; and before a person has achieved realisation, or an insight into this subject, it makes no difference whether he accepts or rejects the existence of *Ātmā*. When we try to give expression to a truth that is beyond thought or expression it becomes only a sort of a symbol which points out a direction or a way through which reality may be known. Buddhism holds that *avidyā* (ignorance) is not the result of the absence of *vidyā* (knowledge), but that it is in fact the opposite of knowledge—a misconception. We ordinary people believe in a self. From the beginning, our consciousness is under the illusion of the independent existence of a self which can be singled out and shown to be individual. Because of this misconception we erect the boundary of 'I' and 'mine'. Whenever the concept of 'I' and 'mine' exists, there is a desire to protect, to possess, to achieve, to know, and so forth. All these are the products of the concept of an individual self which is independent and permanent. When such desire is present it is bound to find an outlet in a number of actions which create karma, both good and bad. Actions attract reactions and so a continuous vicious circle is set up to which there is no end.

In this way and by such actions we take birth, and by taking birth we have engaged ourselves in the processes of disease, decay and death. After death, we shall be reborn and follow the same process; we shall regain the concept of 'I', which once more creates desire, and thus we remain bound and confined within the endless circle in which we are caught and in which we move around senselessly not only from birth to birth but also from day to day. This misconception, which is the thought of self, is always with us whether sleeping or waking and at every moment of our lives. From morning to night we reaffirm a thousand times the illusion which is 'I'. Someone praises us for work well done and immediately we feel proud. Or somebody else abuses us and we feel angry and condemned. In both cases, we feel the self very strongly—or rather the misconception which is the self.

The desire for pleasure and the desire to avoid suffering are ever with us and it is out of these two aspects of the same driving force that all actions are born. For example, if we awake in the morning with a headache, the thought, 'I have a pain in my head', immediately arises. So there is the misconception of the self, expressed in the word 'my' head, followed by a relation between the pain and the self. Then the desire is born to end the pain and this compels us to either take a pill or to see a doctor. Thus this one action starts off a number of other actions in all of which the misconception of self creates other desires and thoughts—such as the preservation of self—and these in turn bring fear which adds to the confusion and conflict.

How can this endless circle be broken? By pushing away one small spoke we cannot stop the movement of a wheel. The centre of the wheel must be broken; the first cause must cease and until that happens, the moving wheel cannot be stopped, its motion can only be suspended for a while. The centre, which is the seed or the first cause, is still there and that means that the second and the third causes can also appear at any time. Therefore, the eradication of misconception, or ignorance, is indispensable if we want to get out of the circle. And the way the wheel is moving circle within circle—involves not only every living being but the entire community of living beings in the world of *samsara*. Each of us moves within our own circle and this combines with numerous others and with numerous other living things. In this way we are bound in collective actions and collective ignorance, which become a part of our own individual karma. The karmic forces and actions of many human beings become intermingled and humanity as a whole is caught in the compelling force of the cycle of *samsara*.

Every person, then, creates his own circle in which he moves out of necessity. The circle combines with, or moves into, other force-centres or circles created by others. All these circles combined engender such a tremendous force that it seems as if we cannot do anything but move around with it and remain helpless until and unless we strike at the root-cause of it all, which is the misconception of self. As the Buddha said: 'The root-cause of misery must be eradicated.' Once we understand misery, we can search for its cause and put an end to it.

The cause of misery, then, is misconception or ignorance, and the direct remedy for ignorance is knowledge—the knowledge of the ultimate truth or *prajñā*. Only when this is realised can ignorance be permanently eradicated. But *prajñā* cannot be realised until there is a stable and one-pointed mind, settled and under command. This stability of mind (*samādhi*) can be brought about through the sustained practice of meditation on one subject only. At the same time, an orderly mind is necessary for the effective practice of meditation. However, to achieve a qualified *samādhi*, we must also have acquired, before and during our meditational practice, good conduct and high moral standards. These perfections make up *śīla*. The three—*śīla*, *samādhi* and *prajñā*—according to the teachings of the Buddha, are interdependent. *Samādhi* is related to *śīla,* as it puts the activities of the body and the tongue in order. Only when *samādhi* has been achieved can we search deeply into the reality of phenomena and realise the wisdom which is *prajñā.*

Śīla is like a body. For example, if we have to cut down a tree, we need a sharp axe. But we also need a good physical body and a strong hand; otherwise we will not be able to use the axe. *Śīla* may be likened to a healthy body, *samādhi* to the strong hand, and *prajñā* to the sharp axe. If these act together, the tree of ignorance can be cut down.

We have talked much about *śīla*, *samādhi* and *prajñā,* and discussed systems and methods of meditation. It may seem as if these teachings are on such a high level that it is impractical to incorporate them into the lives of ordinary people. Therefore it is important to consider how this can be done. It is unlikely that any of us will be able to give up our social obligations and escape from the world, or retire into a jungle in order to meditate until nirvana is achieved. Indeed, to do so could be a sort of cowardice. On the other hand, bravery is called for in order to live a normal life, to continue to practise *śīla*, *samādhi* and *prajñā* and, all the while, to remain pure. Let us consider how to achieve this.

First of all I suggest that each one should draw up a plan for himself and strictly adhere to it. This should be centred around the practice of *śīla*, *samādhi* and *prajñā,* and we should take great care that whatever we do should be in accordance with it. In this way, whatever we undertake will be done in order, whether we are dressing ourselves, walking in the street, or eating food—whatever it may be, will be the action that embodies the tightness of order. Anyone who is aware before he undertakes an action, whether it is in order or not (that is, whether it is right or wrong), lives a disciplined life. This discipline is *śīla*.

Discipline also means that we should concentrate our whole mind on whatever we are doing at the moment—washing, eating or speaking—and that we should keep it collected and never allow it to become scattered or discouraged. Our mind is little accustomed to paying attention to what we are doing; usually, only half of it is on the work or action on hand while the rest is scattered over many other things. Discipline can never be imposed by any outside agent—by religion or another person. It must come from within ourselves with the aid of whatever knowledge, experience and wisdom we have. To give constant attention to every part of our work and to keep the mind recollected at all times is to practise *samādhi*. We may, perhaps, not be able to meditate at a very high level, but we can be careful and attentive in regard to whatever we do; we should never do anything without giving it the full attention of the mind and then every act will manifest reason and wisdom.

Thus, even writing a letter to a friend requires order. First, we write our address and then the date. Then in the letter itself we pay attention to the style of our writing and the correct use of words. And when the letter is finished we read it over to see whether it properly conveys our thoughts, and at the same time we look out for spelling mistakes and so forth. In doing this, a certain care and judgement are needed, especially with regard to the contents of the letter.

There is nothing that cannot be improved and no one is perfect. It does not matter how great an expert a person may be in his field, there is always room for improvement and it is always possible to gain greater knowledge. Therefore we should constantly try to do whatever it is we are doing, whether it be only washing up or putting the house in order, better than before. If this state of constant, undistracted attention is maintained, even to the smallest detail in our life, we shall also grow in insight and wisdom.

When we practise the qualities of care and judgement in our daily lives a new energy is generated in the mind. This is because of the self-discipline, concentration and the endeavour to develop deeper insight into the particular nature of the work. In this way, a steady and gradual development will take place in our character and mind and, as time progresses, we shall be enabled to meditate better and with greater ease, and we shall also gain a better insight into the truth of things.

If we give proper thought to the matter, we shall come to see that a great number of improvements can be made in the way we live and that we can make better use of our time so that the energy and time we spend on prayer, meditation and so-called religious activities and disciplines will not be wasted.

Thought requires lot of inner energy. Therefore when we concentrate on the task in hand we automatically eliminate a great number of thoughts. In addition to that, we could very easily practise in our leisure time emptying our mind of all thought. This can be done when we are lying down after a meal, by not only relaxing our body but also our mind. Let the mind be empty without thought or concentration. The best method to stop thought is to watch it. Usually we never watch our thoughts; we always concentrate on the subject we are thinking about and thus look at the thoughts from the outside only. But if we watch our thoughts coming in and how they progress, they will, as it were, be more hesitant to enter. We might say that they are shy and do not like being watched! This emptiness greatly improves the mind even though this improvement cannot be compared with that achieved by meditation. For those who cannot eliminate thoughts by watching them there is a second method. This is to push all incoming thoughts in a certain direction by giving them a well-defined project or a worthwhile spiritual subject to ponder. We shall find that as soon as we give definite direction to our thoughts, certain difficulties will arise because the mind wants to spread itself over all sorts of subjects and objects rather than follow the specific direction it is given. So we must really concentrate and bring the mind back again and again until it stays with the subject chosen, which may be 'how to serve others', or 'how to be more gentle and affectionate'.

Both of these practices will help considerably even in the midst of living an ordinary life in the world. If people would only experiment with it, they would find out for themselves that even after a week or so definite change takes place.

Another point which I should like to bring to your attention is that we should reduce our hopes and fears because these two types of activities are most disturbing for the mind. Everybody knows that to fear something is not going to help us to escape it when it comes. Nor will hope compel that to happen which is not going to happen. Thus fear and hope are useless activities for the mind. For example, let us watch ourselves waiting for a train. Both fears and hopes disturb us. We keep on looking at the clock to see whether the train will be on time or not; we are suddenly afraid that we may have left something important at home or that our luggage may be lost or stolen. Then, when the train comes rolling into the station we hope to find a good porter and a good seat near the window and a good berth. And during the journey, perhaps, we check at every station whether the train is running on time and worry about whether or not we shall catch our connection at another station. Even though we know that our fears and hopes do not make the slightest difference one way or the other, we continue to entertain them sometimes to the extent of troubling our fellow passengers and making them feel uneasy as well. Similar situations repeat themselves again and again in life. We worry about all kinds of things and try to run away from them or suppress them and so disturb our mental stability. It may be worthwhile reminding ourselves that if there is a remedy for a problem, then there is no need to be fearful or worried, and if there is no remedy then fear and hope are of no use at all and we might as well give them up. It is best to stop worrying and let whatever has to happen do so in its own way.

Our energy should be used in a deliberate manner so that every drop of it achieves something useful. We should always try to conserve our energy because then we can gradually achieve some sort of meditation. Even though we do not meditate sitting down in a certain posture or practise in a set manner, there is the other way of practising it at every moment of our life. If we follow the latter method we can look forward to the development of an insight and wisdom which will transform and enlighten us. And once we have achieved this state of enlightenment in which we realise the truth of selflessness, we shall be free from desire, because once the self is dissolved desire automatically disappears. Desire is always related to self, so if there is no self there will be no desire. Desire is always the action which goes out to serve self, to obtain things for it. So if desire is eliminated there will be no self-centred action. When self-centred action comes to an end, there will be no reaction either. At this point the reverse movement of the vicious circle begins. However, the force of the actions already taken will still have to work themselves out. But when their motion slows down and no new wrong actions are undertaken, because one has realised the truth of selflessness, then the circle of misery will come to an end.

I would like to request you to be mindful of the misery in the universe in general and of all living beings in particular. Be mindful and aware of it; feel it! By feeling it, you will develop loving-kindness and compassion for all sentient beings, and to the extent that compassion unfolds within you, your delusion of self will decrease. Thus your relationship with all other living beings will become more pure and your wisdom will deepen and grow stronger. These two qualities of compassion and loving-kindness in a person indicate that he is beginning to develop spiritually. Perhaps, at first, he will show them in small ways but later he will embrace the whole universe.

I think that the simplest and easiest way to apply our minds to meditation is, first of all, to collect the mind, gather it in such a way as to keep away all kinds of thought. Then, concentrate it and make it one-pointed in comprehending the misery which is experienced by all living beings in the universe, remembering that as we ourselves do not like misery, so other living beings do not like it either. Therefore it is our obligation to do something towards its elimination.

If we can do little at present, we can build up the power of the mind because it is the mightiest power in the universe, for everything was and is created by it. This power cannot be disturbed or challenged by material powers because they themselves are only a by-product of the power of the mind.

Therefore the powers of compassion and wisdom are much stronger than the powers of ignorance and hatred. This being so, we should fill our minds with compassion, loving-kindness and wisdom and radiate these to all living beings together with a strong wish for their happiness.

Never forget to send out the force of loving-kindness to all sentient beings.

GLOSSARIAL INDEX